Cont

THE A-Z OF CURIOUS COUNTY LIMERICK

SHARON SLATER

This book is dedicated to the memory of Sylvia and Dean Mosely.

First published 2021

The History Press
97 St George's Place, Cheltenham,
Gloucestershire, GL50 3QB
www.thehistorypress.co.uk

British Library Cataloguing in Publication Data.
A catalogue record for this book is available from the British Library.

978 0 7509 9503 0

Typesetting and origination by Typo•glyphix
Printed and bound in Great Britain by TJ Books Ltd.

R

S

T

U

V

W

Acknowledgements

I would like to express my deep gratitude to Nicola Guy and the staff of The History Press for giving me the opportunity to share some interesting stories of Limerick's history with the world through this publication.

I am particularly grateful for the assistance given by Dr Matthew Potter and the staff of the Limerick Museum, for their wonderful images of Limerick and the fantastic research carried out in their office.

I would like to offer my special thanks to Jacqui Hayes and the staff of the Limerick Archives, and Mike Maguire and the staff of the Limerick Library, for making a great deal of their collections available online. This is an invaluable asset to this researcher as I could utilise thousands of documents from the comfort of my own home.

I wish to acknowledge the help provided by Alan English and Eugene Phelan at the *Limerick Leader* for allowing access to their back issue and photographic collection.

Thank you to the following individuals and companies for their wonderful images for this publication: Steve Ludlow, Donal Stundon, Eugene Barry, Liam O'Brien, Ann Marie Kennedy, Trish Chester, Presentation College Windsor, National Library of Ireland, *Limerick Leader*, Wouldham Parish Council, The Library of Congress, New York Public Library, New York Parks Department and the National Museum of New Zealand.

The advice given by William O'Neill, Thomas Mulcahy and Catherine Slater during the editing process proved invaluable and I am extremely grateful for their time.

I also wish to acknowledge the amazing Limerick history work carried out by Liam Irwin, Kevin Hannan, Jim Kemmy, Randal Hodkinson, Maurice Egan, David Bracken, Limerick Diocese Office, Lindie Naughton, *Old Limerick Journal* and Limerick historians too numerous to name.

My special thanks are extended to Beline Chan, Sarah Kiely O'Shaughnessy, Deirdre Martin, Lizanne Jackman and Sinead Hanrahan for keeping me entertained throughout this process.

And finally I would like to express my very great appreciation to my family, Susan Mosely, Stephen Clancy and Peter Clancy, for their continued love and support. Also, for giving me the space in our busy lives to put this book together.

Introduction

Limerick not only instils curiosity by its very name, but it also gives a poetic lilt that almost always verges on the humorous. This book does not recount the usual curious tales of Limerick, such as the women who defended the walls during the sieges of the 1690s; no, not even that of the patron saint who cursed the inhabitants of Limerick city. Instead, this volume offers a smorgasbord of short, unique and lesser known stories from Limerick city and county. Here you will discover stories from the curiously questionable to the outright bizarre.

You will also find within these pages some captivating tales that have placed Limerick at the centre of historical events. Such as the daughter of a Limerick family growing up to become the Queen of Corsica; or the salacious tale of two young Limerick women running away together. Not to mention the humorous accounts of Limerick inventors and their strange and pioneering devices, such as a pair of shoes that allowed men to walk on the Shannon River.

The book also dives into some of the unusually named streets of the city and towns in the county, with places such as Effin and Hospital continuing to baffle visitors to the area even today. There are stories of the many city streets named after various Lord Lieutenants of Ireland to gain favour with these high-ranking officials.

There are several other tales that could have been included in this publication, but space dictated otherwise. Stories including the Limerick doctor William Brooke O'Shaughnessy, who introduced cannabis for medicinal purposes into the Western world; or how, before moving to a purpose-built chapel in 1748, the Roman Catholic parishioners of St Mary's in the city worshipped in a malt house; and, the underwater exploits of a former Limerick teacher, John P. Holland, who was a submarine pioneer and supplied his craft to the US Navy.

Also missing is the story of Michael 'Galloping' Hogan, an epic tale of chivalry and defiance. Hogan was born in Doon and following the Cromwellian conquest of Ireland he became a hired bandit. In 1690, he guided Patrick Sarsfield and 500 Jacobites to the Williamite siege train at Ballyneety, where Hogan lit the fuse that blew up the train, slowing the Williamite attack on Limerick. Following the signing of the Treaty of Limerick in October 1691, Hogan became one of the Wild Geese and continued to fight across Europe.

In May 1712, he contributed to the victory of the Portuguese Army against the Spanish at the Battle of Campo Maior. He remained in Portugal until his death and reared a distinguished family, where descendants still live to this day. The story of Galloping Hogan is just one of the 14,000 soldiers who left Ireland in 1691 and spread their wings as far afield as Cuba and South America. This exodus is commonly known as the Flight of the Wild Geese.

And there is no room for stories such as the one reported in the *Nation* newspaper in 1923 about the last recorded case of a woman being legally burned to death in Ireland. It apparently took place in Limerick on 23 April 1768, when Alice Moran met her fate for poisoning Joan Sullivan. While interesting, unfortunately no further information could be found.

Nonetheless, the tales that have made it to the pages are just as interesting, and indeed as strange, and will hopefully give the reader insights into the weird and wacky history of Limerick city and county.

This book goes on a journey through the alphabet, presenting unique and bizarre tales in the A–Z of Curious Limerick, City and County.

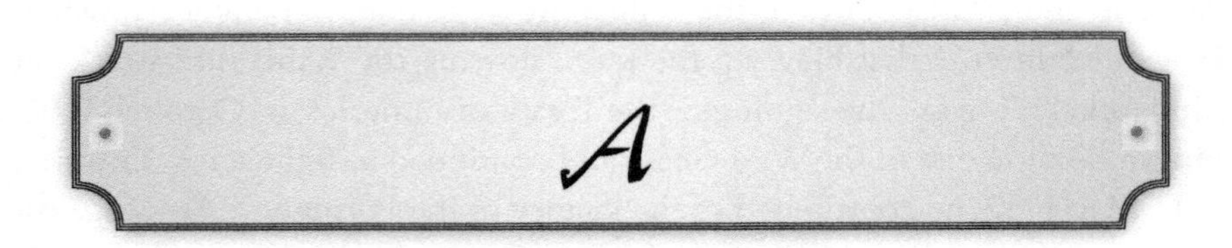

ANIMALS AND THEIR AWESOME ANTICS

Sometimes the antics of animals can be far more entertaining than their human counterparts. The Internet is filled with videos of humorous creatures amusing the masses. Long before the Internet, there are records of people being filled with joy at seeing animals in peculiar settings or acting in an adorable fashion.

The morning of Friday, 6 September 1867 began like any other day in Limerick with workers busying about their day. It was certainly not on the agenda to have a hunt that day, and a chase through the city was unquestionably not on the cards. Despite this, a young deer visiting the property of Mrs Hartigan had a different idea. The fawn, through a series of accidents, set in motion a great chase that day.

This fawn was a regular visitor to Mrs Hartigan's land at Courtbrack. At the time Courtbrack lay at the edge of the city, surrounded by countryside, and it was this countryside that the fawn called home. The edge of the city, far from busy residential areas, was also the perfect location for the kennels of the Limerick Harriers. The land gave the hounds plenty of room to roam free and kept the associated barking and baying from disturbing the public.

On this fateful day, several of the dogs spotted the animal in a nearby field. Their noses perked, and their desire grew. These hounds were trained for the chase. They broke loose from their tethers and gave chase towards the city docks. At the docks they lost sight of the young fawn; it had successfully evaded the pursuers.

The hounds were confused, sniffing at the ground and air, attempting to locate their prey. Incidentally, it was at this very time and place that another deer, this one owned by a Mr Keayes, caught the attention of the hounds. What he was doing with a deer in the city is unclear, but these hunters cared not for the reasons.

To them it was a continuation of the chase, begun minutes before. Keayes' deer lifted its head and piqued its ears at the perceived imminent danger. It immediately set off into flight. It raced up towards Hartstonge Street, circled around Pery Square, back down Barrington Street and into the Crescent. The terrified deer continued running down George's Street (hereafter the references to George's Street will use the modern street name, O'Connell Street). Both stray and pet dogs from around the city joined in the race. People of all ages were looking with bewilderment and confusion. Many also joined the chase alongside their four-legged friends.

The petrified deer set aim towards the city centre, but as the crowds gathered in front of it, the terrified animal turned into Roches Street. The entire spectacle of creatures circled Roches Street, Catherine Street and Glentworth Street three times before the hunt finally came to an end. Miraculously, the deer was rescued from the baying dogs and growing crowd.

This was not the first, nor the last, 'wild goose chase' around the city. It was a warm market day in Limerick on 20 August 1918. Farmers from all over the district were herding their animals through the city from all directions. As the day drew on, the numbers of animals dwindled as the buyers marched their new purchases home, and by five o'clock in the evening the streets were busy with workers finishing for the day. They would never have anticipated the terrifying sight that was about to greet them.

A bull was tied up on Lord Edward Street as its owner was carrying out some business. Suddenly, the beast stirred violently and broke free from its bindings. In a bid for freedom, the bull ran amok through the street. Several people avoided being gouged by the beast by jumping into the nearest house. Eventually, the bull wore itself out in Limekiln Lane, near Sarsfield Barracks. It was here that several men managed to rein in the maddened beast.

Another chase took place in Abbeyfeale in 1931. This one was not as intense as the deer or the bull but perhaps more interesting, as the residents of the town had never seen a creature like it before. During the night of 15 May, a resident of the town awoke to the sight of a peculiar-looking animal in their bedroom. The person in their slumber assumed it to be a Manx cat and managed to chase it from their room.

The following morning, the creature, which was the size of a rat, was spotted in the back of a drapery. The owner of the store attempted to catch the creature, but it escaped out the door. It ran up a tree, where it remained until members of the community began to poke it with a large pole. It was knocked to the street, where it was sadly savaged by a small Kerry blue terrier.

Such was the oddity of the creature that an inquest was held to attempt to identify it. After some in-depth investigation, it was discovered the small animal was an opossum. The American marsupials had escaped from Duffy's Circus two weeks earlier.

There were other strange beasts roaming the Limerick countryside over the centuries. In 1838, three extremely large cats were spotted on Cragg Woods near Askeaton. The local wood ranger was attacked by the felines and narrowly escaped with his life. This attack alerted Mr Cahill of Whiskey Hall near Shanagolden to the danger in his community. He armed himself with a gun and went on the hunt. Cahill located and shot the cats, which were larger than a medium-sized dog. The cats' hides were sent to the Royal Cork Institute, where they were inspected. The Royal Cork Institute ran from 1803 until 1885, when it closed due to lack of funds.

Back in the city in early 1909, the residents of St John's Parish were wise to arm themselves with umbrellas despite the fine weather. A hawk with a wingspan of over 3ft had taken up residence in the area and had a habit of attacking unsuspecting passers-by. The Limerick Bird Fanciers offered a reward of a guinea for the hawk, dead or alive. A cheer rose in the area when a

In 1973, postman John O'Sullivan in Patrickwell's cat had kittens and his dog also had pups. Sadly, the dog was unable to provide milk for her pup so the cat nursed it instead. (*Image courtesy of* Limerick Leader)

Mr Kennedy of Dooradoyle took up the challenge, and he took aim at the feathered foe with his shotgun in Clare Street. The dead bird landed in the Good Shepherd Convent (now the Limerick School of Art and Design), where Kennedy retrieved it.

APOLLO 13 ASTRONAUTS

The entire population of Limerick was glued to its televisions or radios on 11 April 1970, as Apollo 13 launched for the stars. It was to be NASA's third mission to the Moon. This launch did not go as expected and James A. Lovell, John L. Swigert and Fred W. Haise found themselves stuck in space, hit with a series of problems, and uttering those infamous words, 'Houston, we have a problem …'

Although a Moon landing was out of the question, getting the spacemen home proved just as nerve-wracking for those on Earth. Through feats of ingenuity from both those on the ground and in orbit, all three men returned home in one piece.

The men, once recovered, began a worldwide tour to tell of their astral exploits. One of the scheduled stops was in Limerick. On Thursday, 15 October 1970, Lovell, Haise and Swigert landed at Shannon Airport and spent the night in Dromoland Castle, recovering from a somewhat shorter journey than that to which they were accustomed.

The following morning the spacemen travelled by motorcade through the main streets of the city before stopping at the City Library in Pery Square. This library is now the Limerick Gallery of Art. The special guests were treated with a civic reception held by Mayor J.P. Liddy.

The day before, the mayor appealed to the principals of all the city schools to allow students time off to greet the astronauts. This request was granted, and the crowds were so large that is was difficult for the men of honour and two wives to make their way into the library.

The students were baying for autographs and one lucky student from St Munchin's College, 15-year-old Brian English, chatted with the astronauts for several minutes. Lovell spoke for the three astronauts and, after thanking the mayor and the citizens for the fine welcome, he mentioned that he hoped to return to Limerick for a longer stay. He ended by reciting a limerick he had penned for the occasion:

In Limerick, our European tour ended,
And the people a warm welcome extended,
And indeed through Mayor Liddy
In charge of your fair city,
Our hearts to you are surrendered.

THE AMAZING AVIATRIX

Catherine Sophia Pierce-Evans, known simply as Mary, was born on 17 November 1896 in Knockaderry House, near Newcastle West. Traditionally, her fate would be set as the daughter of a wealthy family, where she would be raised to become the wife of a man of means, but there was nothing conventional about Mary's life.

Her father, John Pierce, added the Evans to his name to become heir to his maternal uncle, Thomas Evans. He had not taken a well-to-do wife, but instead his eye fell on a servant, Kate Theresa Dowling. The pair married, and Mary followed soon after. Her parents' marriage was brief and turbulent. While Mary was still an infant, her father hid the small child in a bag and took it with him on a journey to Cork by train. He was soon apprehended by police and returned to Limerick. The community was shocked but not surprised when a few short months later her father murdered her mother. John Pierce-Evans pleaded guilty due to insanity and was imprisoned in Dundrum Mental Asylum for the Criminally Insane. With that, Mary was left an orphan.

The young girl became the ward of her paternal grandparents and was raised by two spinster aunts in Newcastle West. Her tragic upbringing did not stop there, as she also lost her grandparents and her father during her teenage years.

The upbringing Mary had would have undoubtedly ended up given the young girl a sense of independence that was not common for the time. She was well-educated, having attended schools in Cork and Belfast before enrolling in the Royal College of Science in Dublin, earning a degree in Science, specialising in Agriculture.

She was fond of adventure and worked as a dispatch rider for the War Office relaying messages across England and France during the First World War. Mary was also very athletic and was a founding member of the Women's Amateur Athletic Association. She became Britain's first women's javelin champion and set a world record for the high jump.

Despite all these noteworthy achievements, Mary became famous through aviation, when she became the first woman in Britain to hold a commercial flying licence, as well as the first woman to parachute from an aeroplane. In 1928, she became the first pilot, male or female, to fly a small open-cockpit aircraft from Cape Town, South Africa, to London.

Her personal life was similarly rather remarkable. In 1916, Mary met and married Captain William Davies Eliott Lynn, who was twice her age. They were together nine years before divorcing. Her second marriage, in 1927, to 72-year-old Sir James Heath gave her the title of Lady Mary Heath. While the relationship ended in divorce three years later, she kept the name even after her final marriage to Trinidadian jockey and pilot Gar Williams. This sparked a new controversy for the Limerick woman, as a mixed-raced marriage was extremely unusual.

In the air she continued to beat the 'flyboys' at their own game until 1929, when her aviation career suddenly ended following a near-fatal accident in Cleveland, Ohio. Despite this, she remained interested in aviation and the

The amazing aviator Lady Mary Heath and her third husband, Gar Williams, in front of *The Silver Lining*. (*Image courtesy of Lindie Naughton*)

advancement of women pilots until her tragic death in 1939. At only 42 years old, she collapsed on the stairs of a double-decker tram, hitting her head. She died soon after being taken to hospital. Her husband, Gar, scattered her ashes in the most apt way possible for the amazing aviatrix; he spread them through the sky over Surrey while flying an aircraft.

Limerick has another titled aviation expert. In 1988, Adare-born Austin Murphy was knighted by Queen Beatrix of the Netherlands for his work for over twenty-five years as manager of the KLM airline.

On 13 April 2020, during the lockdown for the Covid-19 outbreak, another young deer made its way into the city. It stopped at Sarsfield Bridge and became trapped behind the railing of the 1916 monument.

B

THE BARON OF BROADWAY

How much money would it take for the British Government to sell Northern Ireland to allow for a reunited Ireland? In 1955, Limerick man John J. Hanley attempted to get an answer to this question. Hanley was born a few miles outside Newcastle West, but his life stretched much further than would have been anticipated. As with many Irish citizens before him, Hanley looked out west for his fame and fortune. He landed in New York, where despite the Wall Street Crash and the Great Depression, he became a very wealthy man by running a speakeasy that sold bootleg alcohol.

He became a well-known eccentric figure, rarely seen without his signature diamond-tipped walking cane, and was dubbed Baron Hanley or the Baron of Broadway. Hanley did not drive and on each returning visit to Ireland, he would hire a local as a chauffeur to drive one of his luxury cars that he had shipped for his visit.

Hanley became, unsurprisingly for the time, obsessed with the reunification of Ireland. On several occasions during the 1940s, he was driven across the border to Northern Ireland in a car painted green, white and orange to announce himself as a potential buyer for the six counties. It is not surprising that his offers were not taken seriously in Stormont, but this did not deter the Baron of Broadway.

Finally, in 1955, he decided to go straight to the source. He and his driver crossed the Irish Sea in the custom-painted automobile. He drove through the English countryside, receiving many curious looks on his way to the home of the British Prime Minister at 10 Downing Street. Here he would make an offer in the millions, an offer that the government could surely not refuse. Yet, refuse they did. Hanley left defeated for the final time. His attempts to reunite the country were all in vain.

THE BELLS OF A BUSINESS PAST

In 1980, the clothing store Penneys bought the former Cannock's Department Store building on O'Connell Street and ended an era. The history of Cannock's stretches all the way back to 1850 when John Arnott and George Cannock purchased the drapery business of Cummin and Mitchell. The building was constructed prior to 1800 by Christopher Meade and operated as a drapery from its inception.

In 1858, the clothing factory owner Peter Tait bought out Arnott's share of the company. This was an interesting move as Tait had worked as an apprentice for Cummin and Mitchell when he first arrived in Limerick as a 16-year-old boy. Tait demolished the old building and built a magnificently ornate drapery store, although the clock tower was not erected during this rebuild. Tait left the business abruptly following his bankruptcy in 1869. The store continued to trade under Cannock's name even though it was taken over by James Tidmarsh and Michael Cleary, who later opened Cleary's of Dublin.

The impressive Cannock's lock tower, O'Connell Street, was erected in 1888. This tower was replaced in 1961 when the entire building was renovated. (*Image courtesy of National Library of Ireland*)

In 1888, Cleary was also responsible for expanding the building and erecting the famous Cannock's clock tower. The clockmakers were Gillett and Bland of Croydon and they inserted the four clock faces, with each dial standing 6ft in diameter into the newly constructed tower. Inside, five bells rang the notes of A, D, C, G and F to mark the passing of time. In the decades before the radio, the correct time was taken from a ship's chronometer in Wallace's jewellers on O'Connell Street.

The iconic sights and sounds of these bells in the Limerick streets would stop in 1961 when they rang for the last time. That year the entire building, including the clock tower, was demolished and the building that stands today was constructed. The old hand-wound clock and its chimes did not suit the modern electric era. The last man to wind the clock, Jack Gleazer, would no longer have to climb the 180ft tower, ascending three sets of stairs, and two ladders, to amend the time as he had done for the previous thirty-three years. No longer would he silence the chimes each night by hand; instead an electronic motor would replace the man. As for the bells themselves, they were bought by a Dublin bell founders, who recast the metal. In 1963, the new bells were sent to missions in Kano, Nigeria.

BEARDED WOMAN OF LIMERICK

It is hard to decipher fact from fiction in the tales of Gerald of Wales, the archdeacon of Brecknock, Wales. While on a grand tour of Ireland in the 1180s, Gerald visited Limerick. On his return to Wales, he wrote *Topographia Hibernica* about his travels during this period. His tales were full of fancy and far-fetched notions. One of his tales included meeting a 'Bearded Lady' while staying in Limerick.

Gerald described her as having a 'beard down to her navel'. According to him, she also had a hairy 'crest, like a one-year-old colt'. This supposedly stretched from the top of her neck and ran down her backbone. He went on to describe how the right side of her face was fully bearded like a man, while the left side of her face was soft and smooth like a woman. She was said to live in the court of the King of Limerick, where she was an object of ridicule, as well as wonder.

Despite this bizarre tale, Gerald does give some insight into Limerick of the twelfth century, and he was the first person to mention the walls of Limerick. He described the arrival in 1175 of the Anglo-Normans to the city. Only twenty years later the Anglo-Normans were ousted by the native Hiberno-Norse occupants of the city.

THE BLIND CARETAKER OF ST MICHAEL'S GRAVEYARD

The caretaker of a graveyard should be someone who shows compassion for both the living and dead, be mindful of the surrounding and most of all be able to see. In 1942, a very irate A.J. O'Halloran wrote to the *Limerick Leader*. He was complaining about the condition of St Michael's Graveyard.

The original graveyard surrounded a church of the same name that sat outside the old walls of Limerick for centuries. It was first referred to in the *Black Book of Limerick* in 1205. The church was dismantled during the Cromwellian siege of 1651, but the graveyard remained as a Roman Catholic place of burial until the early twentieth century.

O'Halloran called the graveyard a 'rendezvous for gangs of hooligans'. In his letter, he spoke of the former caretaker, who had died about thirty years earlier. He explained that he had been both blind and deaf, and as a result, he could not keep a watchful eye on the graveyard. This unnamed caretaker was supposedly the last town crier in the city. According to Halloran, he received both positions after losing his sight and hearing in an explosion at the gas works.

Today the entrance to this ancient graveyard is virtually hidden, tucked away by the entrance of a multi-storey car park off Michael Street. It is now under the care of the Limerick Civil Trust, who have maintained the site to a high standard.

St Michael's graveyard, Michael Lane, is now maintained by the Limerick Civic Trust. The oldest legible headstone reads 'Pray for the soul of Catherine Barry of Dunvion who departed this life Feb 12, 1766 aged 92 years'. (*Author's collection*)

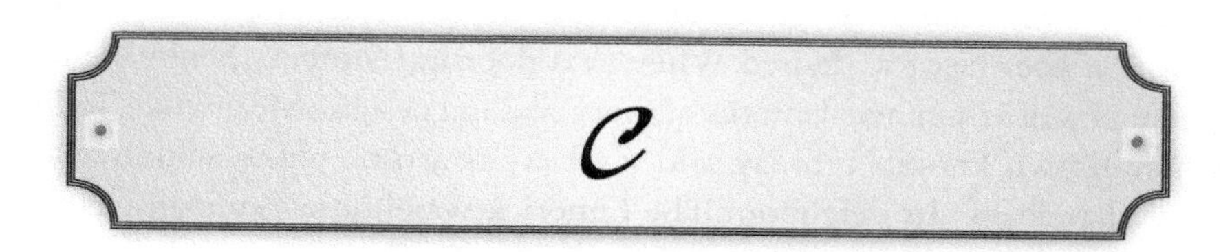

CHRISTMAS IN THE COUNTY

Today families throughout Limerick enjoy their own personal Christmas traditions as well as those passed down through generations. Still, many of the older traditions have gone the way of their practitioners and passed on. In the 1930s a project was launched in the schools throughout the country in which children were encouraged to ask the elderly members of their community about traditions and stories for the *National Folklore Collection*.

Some of the stories recorded by the children included the widely practised tradition of placing a candle in the window on Christmas Eve to denote a welcoming home for travellers. It was also common to leave the door unlocked so the Holy Family could find shelter.

In Kishikirk, Caherconlish, a hollowed turnip decorated with holly and 'fancy paper' was used as a candle holder. In Drumcollogher, in the late nineteenth century, the fire would be left alight and the table would be laid out with food so that those who had passed away could partake in a feast. James Dalton of Athea, born in the 1880s, told a pupil that it was believed that people who died between Christmas Day and Little Christmas were sure to go to heaven.

Meanwhile, in the mid-nineteenth century, a lively story came from Manister. It was said that one Christmas Eve in the town, poteen flowed so freely that a bucket of it was mistaken for water and thrown into the gutters outside the houses. The following morning, Mrs Guare was going to Christmas Mass and saw some ducks drinking from the gutters. To her amazement, she witnessed the ducks become inebriated and waddle around less sure-footed than usual.

The tradition of window shopping was just as appealing, if not more so in 1888. In the run-up to Christmas that year a journalist from the *Limerick Chronicle* described some of the wares on display in the local stores.

In McBirney's, on the corner of Sarsfield Street and O'Connell Street, you could get your hands on 'seal mantles, fur-lined cloaks, plush dolmen and jackets' if your heart so desired. While next door in Cannock there were toys galore as well as 'Chinese lanterns of every size and design'. Meanwhile, Todd's, where Brown Thomas is today, sold 'a variety of artistic photo albums, work boxes, handbags'. Its neighbour, The Limerick Warehouse Company, had an ornate window display, with 'a grotesque figure of an individual with a damask nose' in one window, which spooked passers-by.

Those who were interested in horses would no doubt have visited Mr Delaney, who had on offer 'hunting costumes, ladies riding habits'. While Mr C. Corneille's establishment had 'useful knick-knacks too numerous to mention'. It may have been more helpful to the public if some of these 'knick-knacks' were described.

Jumping forward a century to 2009, Limerick city erected a unique Christmas tree: a 100ft one made of recycled steel. When figuring out where to display this massive art piece, it was decided that instead of mounting the tree in a prominent on-street position it would be placed on the Shannon River, where it would be easiest to see. The Shannon River, on the other hand, was not a fan of this metallic monstrosity and shortly before the official turning on of the festive lights, the gigantic tree fell free of its moorings. It was quickly swept downstream, where it was stopped by the Shannon Bridge.

The tree was rescued and restored to its position, where it would light the festive season for Limerick over the next few years. Finally, in March 2011, the tree had outstayed its welcome within the Shannon and met its watery end. It took another month to rescue the tree, but this time it was beyond saving and was officially retired.

CRIME AT THE CATHEDRAL

On the thirteenth anniversary of the reign of Pope Pius IX fires lit up the night sky in the city, which could be witnessed as far away as Glin. One of these fires on that June 1877 night emanated from the tower of St Mary's Cathedral.

Earlier that day one of the Roman Catholic Clergymen of St Mary's Parish, accompanied by two men and three women, asked the verger of the cathedral for permission to enter the tower. They claimed they wanted to see the illuminations throughout the city from the highest point. One of the women

The Wren Boys of Askeaton dressed to carry out the traditional St Stephen's Day hunt for the wren in 1971. This festive activity included musicians and the troop would sing. (*Image courtesy of* Limerick Leader)

claimed to be too nervous to climb beyond a certain point and the verger remained with her as the other five ascended the tower.

The women, who smuggled four zinc buckets filled with paper and tar underneath their skirts, along with their male companion set one of these fires atop the tower. After a short time, the group descended and left the cathedral, taking their 'nervous' friend with them. The verger closed the premises for the night and made his way home. He was not long outside the door when he was alerted to a fire at the top of the tower. He rushed up the winding stairs and found the paraphernalia, three of the buckets ablaze on the battlements.

THE CORONER CONNERY

In 1824, Limerick man Edward Downes Connery married Anne Theresa Walsh in St Michael's Church on Denmark Street. His wife was the daughter of Patrick Street jeweller Thomas Walsh, while Connery was in the printing trade. He also claimed to have studied medicine while in Ireland, but this has not been confirmed.

Connery's occupation as a printer took him between Limerick and Dublin. On one of his trips to the capital he became acquainted with the budding temperance movement. Soon after this, he relocated his family to New York, where he continued to spread the word on abstinence. While in New York he studied law with a practising attorney. By 1840, he was working as an editor with the *New York Herald*, a position he would hold for decades to come.

In 1855, while still working at the newspaper, he was elected in a landslide victory to the office of coroner for the city of New York. The night of his election thousands of people lined the streets of his neighbourhood singing his praises.

However, these celebratory times did not last. In 1857, while working as coroner, he was involved in the scandalous trial of Emma Cunningham. Although all the evidence pointed at Cunningham for the murder of her wealthy husband, the botched trial at the hands of Connery had her acquitted.

Connery developed a reputation for listening to gossip and accepting it as fact. This was a terrible trait in a newspaper editor and an even worse one in a coroner. As with a villain in any comic book movie, Connery had a habit of revealing all the evidence to murder suspects. This allowed them time to concoct a viable alibi. Within a year of Cunningham's acquittal, she was back in court in a baby-stealing case.

Despite the backlash from this trial, Connery carried on as the coroner for New York for a number of years. When he passed away in 1870 his funeral was as well attended as his election.

THE CRUMPE FAMILY

On 15 September 1766, Samuel Crumpe was born in Rathkeale, County Limerick. He would spend the end of his adult life tending to the sick of Limerick City. When Crumpe was only 22 years old he was awarded a Medical Doctorate at Edinburgh University. His dissertation argued that scurvy was curable with a good diet.

At the time there were very few doctors in Limerick and even fewer that were dedicated to the care of the poor. Lady Lucy Hartstonge established a hospital in Limerick in 1780 at the old Guard House of the Citadel, in St John's Parish. Crumpe returned to Limerick in 1788 and took up the role of chief physician in Lady Lucy's hospital. There he treated patients with rare and infectious diseases.

While tending those in need, he also continued his research, publishing a book, *An Inquiry into the Nature and Properties of Opium*, in 1793. Although he knew he had to perform tests on animals for his experiments, he endeavoured to use them as little as possible. He also tested his theories on himself, changing the consistency of opium by exposing it to heat and cold, and in liquid form, and he tasted it in various strengths to see if it reduced the natural bitter flavour. His work on opium provided a basis for classifying the drug as a stimulant rather than a narcotic and was the first to provide an extensive discussion of its withdrawal effects. He did not approve of the common practice of bloodletting and believed that wine was a better remedy than opium for reducing general fevers.

In January 1796, Dr Crumpe was out walking when he witnessed a crowd surrounding a woman who had collapsed. He found that she had a fever and had her taken to hospital. Sadly, he contracted her illness and passed away soon after, aged only 29. He was interred in the grounds of St Mary's Cathedral, near the Great West Door.

Although Dr Crumpe died young, he left a legacy in medicine that is still present today. His daughter, Mary Grace Susan Crumpe, also went against the grain, writing historical romances in the 1820s, such as the strangely named *Isabel St. Albe, or, Vice and Virtue* and *Geraldine of Desmond or Ireland in the reign of Elizabeth*. On 16 October 1854, Mary married the extravagantly named Alexander Louis Joseph Count Milon de Villiers, Chevalier of the Legion of Honour, in Dover. Mary died in 1861 in Jersey, childless, and so the direct Crumpe line ended.

St John's Hospital as it looked when it was founded by Lady Lucy Hartstonge in 1780 and Dr Samuel Crumpe worked there. (*Image courtesy of the Limerick Museum*)

DICKENS AND THE DUCKS

Charles Dickens undertook a tour of Ireland in 1858 during the height of a scandal involving his separation from his wife. By the time he reached Limerick on Tuesday, 31 August, this was hot gossip for those attending his performances at the Theatre Royal, Henry Street, Limerick, on Wednesday, 1 September and Thursday, 2 September 1858.

The *Limerick Chronicle* published an article on Wednesday morning, one which Dickens may himself have read as he stayed in Cruise's Hotel. They mentioned that Dickens had separated from his wife in 'consequence of their tempers not agreeing'. They did not condone the married 46-year-old Dickens having a relationship with 18-year-old Ellen Ternan.

Arriving the night before his performance, Dickens had time to write to his nephew, describing Limerick as 'the oddest place of which nobody in any other part of Ireland seems to know anything. Nobody could answer a single question we asked about it.' His letters emphasise that he had a pleasant, albeit strange, stay in Limerick. He told his nephew that he was glad to come to the city, even though he could have made far more money if he had stayed in Dublin.

As he readied for the first performance, where he would read from his most popular tales, he was met with an extraordinary sight. When the doors opened, three ducks rushed into the theatre. Dickens later told his nephew that he expected a pig the following night. Even with the farmyard excitement, Dickens wowed the audience with his characterisation of those characters from *The Pickwick Papers* and *A Christmas Carol*, as well as those from his lesser-known stories.

Despite Dickens' fondness for Limerick, calling the Theatre Royal 'a charming Theatre. The best I ever saw, to see and hear in', the local press continued to lambast him for his marital failings. The editor of the *Limerick*

Cruise's Hotel, O'Connell Streeet opened its doors in 1791. It was the rest stop of choice for Limerick's most famous visitors. Those who stayed there include Charles Dickens, Franz Liszt, John Redmond, the tenor John McCormack, Rock Hudson and the New Zealand All Blacks. (*Image courtesy of the Limerick Museum*)

Chronicle sided with Dickens' wife, asking on 8 September, 'If, in defiance of good taste and common sense, Mr Dickens will persist in obtruding his matrimonial troubles before the public.'

DUTIES OF A DUKE

The Lord Lieutenant of Ireland, the King's representative in the country, was the highest position attainable in Irish politics from 1690 until 1922. Although Lord Lieutenants were appointed for no set period, in practice they were often replaced as each successive government fell.

As these men visited Limerick, they met with the official pomp and ceremony befitting their role. In October 1809, one of these men, Charles Lennox, the 4th Duke of Richmond, arrived in Limerick City. He had been in the role for a year and a half by this time and was taking a grand tour of the country.

He arrived into the city with an extremely large entourage, which included his wife Charlotte, the eldest two of their fourteen children, as well as Lady Somerset, Major Loftus, Captain Ready and Sir Charles Vernon. Meanwhile, the red carpet was rolled out in Limerick by the Earl of Clare, Colonels Vereker and Prendergast Smyth, Major Vereker, the City High Sheriffs and a vast number of citizens.

The party travelled to Bishop's Palace on Henry Street, where they rested for a few hours before dinner that evening in Milford House. The next day, the Duke was presented with the keys to the city by Francis Lloyd, Mayor of Limerick. This was followed by yet another grand dinner.

During another outing, while the Duke was attending to the military, the Duchess visited William Roche's famous gardens. These were built on arched vaults and boasted the widest range of fruits and flowers in the city. This was made possible by a series of climate-controlled greenhouses. Two streets in the city were named in honour of this visit; Richmond Street (now St Joseph's Street) and Richmond Place (now The Crescent).

Other Lord Lieutenants were also immortalised in street names throughout Limerick City and County. The Lord Lieutenant of Ireland in 1798 was Lord Charles Cornwallis, who surrendered to George Washington during the American War of Independence. He gave his name to Cornwallis Street (now Gerald Griffin Street). John Russell, Duke of Bedford, who was appointed Lord Lieutenant in 1806, gave his name to Bedford Row. Charles Manners, 4th Duke of Rutland, appointed Lord Lieutenant of Ireland in 1784, and who visited Limerick in 1785, when Rutland Street was named.

Richard Wellington, Marquis of Wellesley (brother of the Duke of Wellington), Lord Lieutenant in 1823, gave his name to multiple streets, including Wellesley Lane, Wellesley Bridge (now Sarsfield Bridge) and Wellesley Place, (now Clontarf Place). Wellesley Bridge was officially opened in 1835, by the then Lord Lieutenant, Constantine Henry Phipps, the Earl of Mulgrave, after whom Mulgrave Street was renamed.

It is interesting to note that two Lord Lieutenants opened sections of the docks, but neither were immortalised in the city. These were Edward Eliot, 3rd Earl of St Germans, who opened the floating docks on 26 September 1853. In 1873, Earl John Spencer, the great grand-uncle of Princess Diana, opened the graving docks.

DESECRATION OF THE DEAD

When Captain Laurence Durack died in Tarbert in February 1824, his family wanted to honour his wishes to be buried in the churchyard of St John's in the city. This proved to not be an easy task. The family decided to bring their own religious leader to officiate at the funeral. This would not have been an issue except the officiant was a Roman Catholic and St John's was Church of Ireland.

While the graveside service was taking place, the vicar of the parish, John Fitzgibbon, was looking out the window of his home on John's Square. He noticed his sexton running towards the house and enquired the cause of the issue. The sexton responded that McCarthy was performing the rites wearing the full robes of the Roman Catholic Church.

This had sparked anger with some of the local parishioners. Stones were thrown at the funeral attendees, some striking McCarthy. Instead of coming to McCarthy's aid, the vicar insisted that he stop the service immediately. However, the Catholic priest continued his sermon. The vicar found this insulting to his core and called upon the military to remove the priest. This he claimed was his right under the law as the practice of Catholicism was still under prohibition under the Penal Laws. Durack did get interred, but not with the last rites of his chosen church.

This was not the last time that St John's Church in John's Square faced controversy over its treatment of the dead. In June 1851, Rev. John Elmes of St John's Church was under investigation for the desecration of the dead in the churchyard. Rumours led to an investigation by the Mayor of Limerick, Thaddeus MacDonnell.

When the investigating committee visited the churchyard, they found that the greater part had been levelled, an endeavour to make way for the construction of the new St John's Church. The surface contained the remains of human bones in various stages of decay. These uprooted bones, along with the soil surrounding them, had been removed to the old pig market off Mulgrave Street.

It had appeared that the removal of soil containing bones had been taking place for some time to facilitate the erection of the new church. Every section of the churchyard, except the tombs, was under construction, where several coffins were uprooted, some so fragile that they were burned in heaps in the churchyard. In some areas, all traces of the burial place of certain families were obliterated by the removal of the tombstones. These and headstones lay piled over each other, having been removed from their position.

A week after this inspection took place the report was brought up in the Limerick Town Council. One of the members, Mr Cullen, stated that 'it was the duty of the vicar not only to protect the souls of the living, but to take care

Aerial view of St John's Church, Church of Ireland, John Square. In the churchyard a gravestone reads 'Sacred to the memory of Revd John Elmes. The beloved minister of this parish for 31 years. Under whom the present church was rebuilt.' (*Image courtesy of Donal Stundon*)

of the dead, and he would be sorry to hear that any clergyman would act in such a manner as it now appeared the Rev Mr Elmes did'.

The work on the new church and churchyard ended the following year. The Rev. John Elmes continued as rector of St John's Church. He passed away in the rectory at John's Square in 1869 and was buried in the churchyard that had caused so much controversy eighteen years earlier. His epitaph reads, 'Sacred to the memory of Revd John Elmes. The beloved minister of this parish for 31 years. Under whom the present church was rebuilt. He died on Jany 5th 1869 aged 63 years.'

E

THE END OF THE EARL

The 1st Earl of Limerick was born Edmond Henry Pery on 8 January 1758. He was the nephew of Edmond Sexton Pery, who founded Newtownpery, and the son of William Cecil Pery, the Protestant Bishop of Limerick and the 1st Baron of Glentworth.

To say that he was well-to-do would be an understatement. He studied at Trinity College in Dublin before embarking on a tour of Europe. While in France he was introduced to the Court of Louis XVI and became a favourite of the ill-fated household.

Even though he had so much, he was not content and craved more. He wrote to his uncle, Edmond Sexton, on 1 December 1782, asking: '… if it meets with your approbation, it will be of the utmost importance to me if you would write a few lines to Sir Harry expressive of your consent, and if you would also remind him of a promise he made to you of settling his fortune in case I married Miss Ormsby.'

Alicia Mary Ormsby was the niece of Sir Henry (Harry) Hartstonge and was due to inherit his fortune. Hartstonge was also Edmond's uncle by marriage. The marriage proposal between Pery and Ms Ormsby was approved. They went on to have eight children, including Theodosia, who married Thomas Spring Rice, immortalised on the top of a pillar in the People's Park.

Following in his uncle Edmond Sexton's footsteps, Edmond Henry became a career politician, holding offices such as Keeper of the Signet and Privy Seal of Ireland, Clerk of the Crown and Hanaper of Ireland. Following the Act of Union in 1800, he became a representative peer, sitting in the House of Lords for forty-three years.

On Saturday, 7 December 1844, following a protracted illness, the news broke of the death of the Earl at his home in South Hill Park, Berkshire. He was 87 years old. In the days following his death, his body was laid out at his home in a room carpeted with black cloth.

Subsequently, as his body was returned to his ancestral home, his funeral was not met with the civility and courtesy anticipated after the loss of such a notable figure in Limerick history. Instead, the streets were filled with rioters, who harassed the mourners as they made their way through the city.

Why was the Earl so disliked in his home city? This stems from his political affiliation as a vocal Unionist. He was extremely anti-Catholic and denounced the 'active machinations of the Popish priesthood'. In the last ten years of his life, although he had retired from actively participating in politics, he would still attend the House of Lords to give his vote in person 'against every piece of Irish policy that savoured of O'Connellism' (followers of Daniel O'Connell).

The tide had turned against Protestant control in Limerick and O'Connell campaigned for the rights of Irish Catholics. For this he was known as the Liberator, or the Emancipator, making him overwhelmingly popular in Limerick. In contrast to the Earl, following O'Connell's death, a statue was raised, and streets were renamed in his honour.

In 1844, Limerick was struggling financially, and although this was before the famine, poverty was rife. The rights of Catholics were at the fore in local politics. Unsurprisingly, the return of the Earl, who opposed Catholic emancipation, was not met with the solemn decorum expected at a funeral.

As his remains began their long journey back to Limerick, the Pery family took the opportunity to repatriate the remains of his father, William Cecil Pery, and Edmond Henry's wife, Alicia Mary, in separate hearses to their ancestral burial vault in St Mary's Cathedral.

As the remains of his family made their way through Clare Street, they were unfortunately mistaken for the remains of the Earl. A gathering crowd began 'hooting and groaning' and continued to do so as they followed the hearses to the cathedral. After the subsequent memorial service, both coffins were then laid in the family vault by torchlight.

Meanwhile, the remains of the Earl passed unhindered in a hearse drawn by six black horses to the Pery home in Henry Street. They laid in state in the back dining room of his family home the following day, when all facets of society came to pay their respects.

Those who remained outside the house were not as mournful. When the coffin was placed in the hearse, this crowd began whistling and jeering, some even attacking the procession, attempting to tear the mourning scarfs from them.

St Mary's Cathedral, Bridge Street was erected in 1168 on the site of the former palace of the O'Brien kings of Thomond which was built on the site of a Viking meeting place also known as a thingmote. (*Author's collection*)

As the funeral procession made its way to St Mary's Cathedral, the boisterous crowd grew in size and volume. They chanted, 'Don't you know he was an enemy to O'Connell, and an absentee.' On reaching the potato market, the mob grew violent, hurling potatoes and apples at the carriages. Some of the mourners, including Thomas Spring Rice, escaped their carriages, seeking refuge in a public house.

Some of the crowd made it into the cathedral, one placing an old hat on the statue of Bishop Jebb. So intense was the scene that the military were called. They arrived within thirty minutes and the mob finally dispersed, allowing the coffin to be brought into the cathedral. A memorial service followed, and the Earl was laid to rest alongside his father and wife.

Despite the drama surrounding his funeral, the Earl left the city a sum of £500 in his will for local charities. This was £100 to the County Infirmary (Regional Hospital), £100 to Barrington's Hospital, £100 to the Fever Hospital (St John's Hospital), £50 to the Protestant Orphan Society, £50 Sisters of Mercy, £50 to the Convalescent Dispensary and £50 to the Presentation Schools.

THE ESCAPE OF ELLEN BROWNE

In 1824, in Birr, County Offaly, Ellen Browne was born, but she moved to Limerick as a young woman. By the time she was 21 years old, she was well known to the city courts. Her first term in the city jail came on 2 September 1844, where she served six months at hard labour for larceny and fourteen days for assault. She fell into her old pattern following her release and was back in jail on 18 August 1845, for stealing clothes from a Mr O'Neill. This was a time of enormous strife in Ireland as the country plunged into famine.

Sentences of transportation to Australia were still common practice and it was unusual that Browne avoided the sentence for as long as she did. Her day finally came when, on 1 November 1845, she was sentenced to seven years' transportation. Unsurprisingly, the 5ft 1in brunette with a large freckle on her forehead was not pleased and decided to take her life into her own hands. On Sunday, 16 November 1845 she managed escaped from the jail. She was wearing a brown dress, whitish handkerchief, brown apron, blue stockings and shoes.

The news spread quickly of her escape. A £3 reward was set for her discovery. Using her wits, she remained undetected for five days. However, she was eventually returned to jail, where she remained for another year. She could not evade the sentence of transportation forever, and on 25 February 1847, after a long three months' travel, she arrived in the penal colony in Australia.

It was not all wretchedness for Browne. In November 1850, she was granted permission to marry another convict, John McCann. Two years later she was released from the prison a married woman on 29 October 1852.

Over fifty years earlier, a strangely reversed episode took place in Limerick. In September 1787, the city was shocked over the murder of weaver Michael Dennesy, also known as Donoghue. The murder suspect, Thomas Hogan, remained at large.

Three months passed, and the case was fading in public memory when Hogan, a clerk, presented himself at the door of the city jail. Once inside he asked for a pen and paper. He used this to post a notice in the local papers informing the prosecutors and the relatives of the deceased that he was now in jail and would appear before the next sitting of the courts. The letter indicated that Hogan planned to clear his name, but it is not known if his plea was successful in the courts.

EXTRAORDINARY ELOPEMENT

On 11 October 1857, two teenage girls from Dromcollogher appeared in a Liverpool police court. The girls, Ellen Fitzgibbon and Catherine Barry, were arrested while on their way to Australia. Their adventure began a week earlier back in Dromcollogher when 16-year-old Ellen and her friend Catherine hatched a plan.

One morning, after packing their finest clothing, the girls decided to elope together. To aid in their journey, Catherine, who was living with her uncle James Barry, broke into one of his safe boxes and stole £40. The girls quickly made their way to Charleville train station where they boarded the next train to Dublin.

Meanwhile, James Barry returned home to find his niece and money missing. He soon discovered that Fitzgibbon was also missing and informed the police. As he was searching the countryside around Dromcollogher, the girls boarded the ferry to England.

With their sights set on Australia, they quickly befriended two young Irish men bound for Australia. Soon, they had spent most of their funds. Their tickets to Melbourne on board the White Star clipper cost them £14 each.

During this time James Barry was continuing his enquiries and discovered that the girls were in Liverpool. He alerted the police there as he made his way across the Irish Sea. His luck was with him and against the girls as they were found on board the ship ready to depart. The girls claimed to be married to their new paramours but as there was no legal agreement or religious ceremony carried out the girls were removed from the ship.

They waited in the police station for their hearing and Catherine's uncle to arrive. During the trial James Barry insisted that he did not wish to see the girls charged with theft; his only objective was to take them back to Dromcollogher. The judge agreed, and the girls were released into his custody.

The girls thanked Judge Mansfield as they left the court. This was the last major foray for the pair as after they returned to Limerick they led rather quiet lives.

ECCLESIASTICAL EVACUATION

In June 1889, a very strange occurrence took place in the parish of Knockea. Some persons unknown climbed through the window of the local chapel, where they proceeded to locate one man's gallery pew, that of Michael Ryan. They continued to physically cut out Ryan's seat and foot rail. After extracting the seat, they discarded them outside the church.

The reasoning behind this wanton destruction was to send a message to Ryan to stop attending the church. A few weeks earlier, when Ryan had entered the church a large portion of the congregation left before the service began. They disagreed with his act of 'land grabbing' after he bought a farm in Ballyneety following the eviction of the widow Clune.

Following the walkout, Rev. Dr Moloney arrived in the parish from Limerick and alerted parishioners that if they were to walk out again the church would be closed by order of the Bishop of Limerick. At the next mass, the congregation did not leave after Ryan entered but others who had seats in the gallery did not take them.

The Bishop once again intervened, calling on those with seats in the gallery to occupy them under the threat of the closing of the chapel. This threat did not have the desired result. Instead it encouraged some members of the parish to carry out the vandalism of the pew on a Friday night. Ryan attended the half past eleven mass on the Sunday and he had to stand or kneel throughout. He was the sole occupant of the gallery.

The mass was attended by six constables from the Drombana Police Station, while another six and a sergeant took up positions in the yard. Following the mass, Fr Crotty told the congregation that the chapel would be closed indefinitely due to the treatment of Ryan and destruction of church property. He announced that no sacraments would take place in the parish barring exceptional circumstances and that children would have to be taken to Donoughmore to be baptised.

After the service ended, Ryan was escorted home by two of the constables. A reward of £10 was offered by the Knockea National League to find the vandals, but the culprits were never located. The chapel remained closed for six months. Ryan did not attend the first Mass after the reopening.

Sketch of Knockea Church which was closed for six months by order of the Bishop of Limerick. Drawing by Peter Clancy. (*Author's collection*)

FOLKLORE AND FAIRY FORTS

In early winter of 1951, three English tabloid newspapers, the *Daily Mirror*, *Daily Telegraph* and *Sunday Express*, reported that fairies were in Limerick. These articles came about after Limerick Corporation began building work in Ballynanty Beg that went through an ancient Ráth or fort. In Irish tradition, these old forts were the homes of fairies, who would protect them with a vengeance.

The tabloids claimed that each night the newly erected walls were dismantled by the fairies. The Corporation was shocked to see these reports, and that the

This image of Grange stone circle ring was taken around 1900 by G. Fogerty and shows the enormous height of the stones in the circle. (*Image courtesy of the Limerick Museum*)

city was becoming a laughing stock. They called for a redaction and apology, which they received from the Irish News Agency. Unfortunately, the damage was already done, and the news of vengeful fairies spread to the other side of the world, where it was reported in Australia.

This was not the first time that Limerick had come up against the English tabloids. In 1887, many newsagents of the city refused to stock 'English periodicals of the sensational type'. This came about after a discussion with the local clergy. The *Nation* cited that it was the newsagents' duty to 'protect the young minds of their children from the moral injury which must certainly result from acquaintance with the gutter literature'. Unfortunately, this ban was not taken up by all and the tabloids continued to flourish.

As for the 'fairy forts', these are dotted all over the county of Limerick. They even lie within the boundary of the city, in the district of Raheen, an area named because of the number of Ráth remaining in the area. Some of these have caused roads to be bent and curved, such as in Maigue Avenue. The superstition was so prevalent that builders refused to upset the ancient formations.

Interestingly, a ring fort at Reerasta, just outside the village of Ardagh, became the home to one of the finest examples of early Christian Irish metalwork. The well-known Ardagh Chalice was discovered in the ring fort in 1868. It was not alone: the hoard also contained a smaller bronze chalice and four silver-gilt brooches.

Other ancient architecture still stands in Limerick, including the largest stone circle in Ireland. This structure in Grange, near Lough Gur is over 4,000 years old. The circle is comprised of a continuous ring of 113 upright stones. Some of these stand up to almost 3m high. The entrance of the circle is aligned with the rising sun at the Summer Solstice. As such, it is the site of an annual pilgrimage for those wishing to witness this remarkable event.

FOWL CRIMES OF A FEMALE FLEECER

The night watchmen of St Michael's Parish were on one of their normal patrols one night in March 1819 when they spotted a hunched figure in the shadows. On inspecting this unusual sight, they found Bridget Geraghty carrying a heavy weight. As they came closer to the woman, feathers appeared from under her cloak. The shocked watchmen questioned her regarding the fowls smuggled beneath her cloak, and finding her answers unsatisfactory, arrested her immediately. They removed her to the station, with her fowl friends in tow.

The next morning, she was taken from the station to the court. Her ill-gotten gains were so large and heavy that they were carried on a pole between two men. She was found guilty of stealing birds from the Lemonfields area. During the trial, it was discovered that she, along with three others, Bridget Lynch, Ellen Day and Patrick Dea, had carried out a stealing spree over the previous four months throughout the county. The gang was responsible for the killing of fifty-three turkeys, 124 geese, 110 ducks, two sheep, and twelve goats. They also stole twelve bags of wheat and twenty-six bags of oats. They hit other farms in the Ardnacrusha, Crossnagalla, Roxborough and Ballyneety. Naturally, she and her gang were convicted by the magistrate, Alderman Watson, and sent to prison.

THE FEMALE FREEMEN

Although there have been many Freemen of Limerick throughout time, the number of female Freemen can sadly be counted on one hand. The first, Ishbel Maria Hamilton-Gordon, Countess of Aberdeen, was honoured on 8 June 1894, by Mayor Bryan O'Donnell. The Countess was heavily involved with Limerick lace and encouraged the revival of this hand craft.

The second was the Irish revolutionary and actress, Maude Gonne. She was honoured on 13 December 1900 by Mayor John Daly. Interestingly, the third woman honoured was Kathleen Clarke, the niece of Mayor Daly. Her late husband, Thomas Clarke, had also received the Freedom of Limerick from Mayor Daly.

Clarke was given the highest honour of the city by Mayor Alphonsus M. O'Mara on 5 September 1918. It would take three years before Clarke would sign her name in the roll of honour. At the same ceremony on 5 December 1921, Eamon de Valera was inducted and Limerick's first female Deputy Mayor, Marie O'Donovan, officiated. O'Donovan was deputised into the role when Mayor Stephen O'Mara travelled to the United States.

In 1993, there was talk of a fourth female Freeman of Limerick. This was none other than Mother Theresa, who was on a visit to the city. She was offered the honour but refused to accept it after the nomination caused controversy with local politicians. The actual fourth was in 1997, when Trudy Hunt received the award with her brother John Hunt, in recognition of the work

The old Town Hall on Rutland Street was built in 1805 by the precursor to the Chamber of Commerce. It was occupied by the Limerick Corporation from 1846 until 1990 when the new City Hall was constructed on Merchant's Quay. (*Image courtesy of the Limerick Museum*)

begun by their parents on cultural heritage, but whose efforts were continued by the Hunt children.

THE FURIOUS FORGERS

In 1809, a case was brought in the Rathkeale petty sessions by a local man called Hanrahan. Hanrahan was suing his neighbour for giving him a forged banknote, which he had tried to exchange but was refused. It was relatively easy to forge banknotes at the time, which was carried out with an engraved plate of the note, or some talented artist employed to copy notes by hand.

In a strange turn of events, several individuals showed up in court that day; not to act as witnesses for Hanrahan, but against him. They accused Hanrahan of selling a 30*s* note for 9*s* and a two guinea note for 3*s*. Hanrahan was immediately arrested and taken to the town jail to appear at the next court sitting.

There were many other cases of forgery throughout the centuries in Limerick and in 1850 another of these caught the public attention. A respectable-looking man in his forties called John Graham, who also went by Henry Dixon, was up in court for forging a plate to create Bank of Ireland £1 notes.

Graham decided to defend himself in the court, and he cross-examined the witnesses and subsequently addressed the jury at considerable length. The witnesses placed Graham at the scene of the crime in Augustinian Lane in the city. It must be mentioned, though, that many of these witnesses had previously been arrested for passing forged notes so were not the most reliable of people.

When the prosecution closed their case, the prisoner stood and addressed the jury with a long-winded speech. When the judge asked if he intended to call any witnesses, Graham replied that he did not. Graham did, however, go on to say, 'My Lord, please inform the jury that there was not any evidence given of the place where the offence was done. I submit, my lord, that there was no evidence given throughout the whole of this case, that the offence was committed in the city of Limerick.'

This caused an audible sigh throughout the court and a back and forth between the sergeant in the court and Graham. The prisoner asserted that although the witnesses had mentioned Augustinian Lane, not one had uttered Limerick afterwards and there very well may be lanes by that name in Waterford, Dublin or Cork.

The judge asked for the arresting officer to return to the court. This made Graham ask, 'My Lord, will your lordship permit me to be put on trial again?' The response was a firm 'no'. He enquired where Augustinian Lane was situated. Once that question was answered, the jury was sent away to deliberate. This they did for half an hour before returning the verdict of guilty.

The judge then pronounced, 'The jury having convicted you of this offence, it becomes my duty to relieve society of a member whose presence in the country would be productive of the most pernicious results.' Graham was sentenced to transportation to Australia for life.

The prisoner responded to this verdict with, 'Very well, my Lord. Now, as I am to be transported for the period of my natural life, I must assert that the twelve gentlemen of the jury have put themselves on an equilibrium with my prosecutors in this plot of multitudinous perjury.'

Graham would remain in prison in Ireland until September 1851, when he was placed on board the ship *Rodney*, destined for Australia.

FIRE! FIRE! FIRE!

Fires have ravaged both Limerick city and county many times throughout history. The most tragic of these occurred on 5 September 1926 in Dromcollogher. It remained the worst-known fire disaster in Irish history until the Betelgeuse incident in 1979. On that heart-breaking day in September, many members of the local community went out to enjoy a film in a timber barn, which was being used as a temporary cinema.

The film used was a reel of nitrate, an extremely flammable substance. When the reel came too close to a spark, it caught light and exploded immediately. It spread rapidly, igniting other film reels in the area, and the entire building was quickly an inferno. Forty-eight people died in this tragedy. Forty-six of the victims were buried in a large grave in the grounds of the local church.

Many tragic fires occurred in the city centre, which destroyed and completely gutted well-known businesses, such as O'Callaghan's tannery in 1950, Todd's in 1959 and Newsom's in 1974. These fires changed the appearance of the city centre as new modern buildings were erected to replace the more classical styles that had been destroyed. Fires in the city were not just a twentieth-century phenomenon.

During the height of the famine, in April 1847, a conflagration on the corner of Thomas Street and Catherine Street destroyed a brush factory and several other buildings in the area. The brush factory, owned by Messrs Egan and McCormack, employed over 250 people. It contained the perfect tinder for such a disaster. When the flames were at their highest, they touched the roofs of thatched cottages on both Roches Street and Catherine Street.

If it was not for the fast action of the city police, Royal Horse Artillery, a troop of the 8th Hussars, fatigue and armed parties of the 55th and 59th Regiments, the Augustinian chapel, where the bell had been rung to summon help, would have been swallowed up by flames. Many citizens, who had taken to their beds as the fire began close to midnight, found themselves with no other choice but to leap to their fate, and many women found themselves in the street in their night dresses. Luckily, all those who escaped the buildings survived, although many were injured. They even managed to rescue two horses before their stable, at the rear of the flames, burned to the ground. Although the building and all its contents were destroyed, the outcome could have been worse for the brush factory, which was insured for £3,000.

Just as this fire was fading from memory, another one erupted to take its place in the limelight. This time the location was Steamboat Quay, where in

November 1863, a large corn store went up in flames. William Cochrane, commission agent, owned the store. The fire grew so intense that it took over the neighbouring store and houses of the City of Dublin Steam Packet Company.

Every fire engine in the city was dispatched, including those of the military, but it was no use. The heat was so intense that two horses and a mule were burned to a cinder. A young lad, Thomas O'Donnell, was watching the inferno when a beam fell and ignited his clothing. He jumped into the river to extinguish the flames, but sadly, this also extinguished his life.

It would not take long for the next fire to hit the city. On the evening of 30 May 1866, one of the employees at Michael Cusack's general merchant store on William Street stood on a box of Lucifer matches. The matches sparked a paraffin cask, causing it to instantly burst into flames. Once again, as history dictates, the fire threatened the entire street.

Several public and private fire engines arrived soon after; these included the Corporation engine, the army engine and engines from the Sun and West of England insurance companies. At the time, individuals could insure their homes and businesses against fire by opting to pay extra for the use of private fire engines. The engine drivers would distinguish these businesses by use of a plaque attached to the front of the building. One of these plaques remains today on a Tontine Building in Pery Square. The *Limerick Chronicle* reported that the 'fire burst with such terrific force that it wrapped the two houses … very rapidly in its flames'.

It was quickly realised that Cusack's building could not be saved, so the process to protect the adjourning premises became the top priority. Panic increased when it was discovered that a large quantity of gunpowder was stored at the rear of the burning building, bringing back memories of the great gunpowder explosion of 1837, which was still in living memory. It became even more imperative that the rescue team moved quickly.

Eventually, the front wall of Cusack's building collapsed, and after four hours, the fire engines stopped, and the owners of the damaged businesses could only survey their losses. Luckily, Cusack and McDonagh were insured by Queen insurance for premises, stock and furniture up to £2,400, while the confectionary store was insured by Sun insurance, which had provided an engine that fought the flames.

The famous Todd's fire exploding out of William Street in 1959. (*Image courtesy of Eugene Barry*)

GHASTLY GUNPOWDER

A few short years after the final siege of Limerick, the city was still home to the military and their accompanying materials. On 12 February 1693, one of the towers that defended the entrance to Merchant's Quay collapsed. Tragically, this building contained 250 barrels of gunpowder. The violent crash of material caused the gunpowder to explode, propelling debris in every direction. Several houses were destroyed, and 210 people were killed or wounded by the blast. The explosion was so intense that it was reportedly felt as far away as Kilmallock.

As the saying goes, it is important to keep your gunpowder dry, but Thomas Spellissy in Thomondgate took that a little too far. On 21 November 1813, Spellissy, a quarryman, was trying to dry gunpowder in an iron pot over an open fire. This was not the wisest decision, as a spark from the open hearth ignited the powder, killing the quarryman instantly. The explosion caused the house to collapse. Spellissy's wife, child, and two other occupants of the house, Michael Conway and Bridget Enright, were buried under the rubble for over an hour. While the three adults were rescued, the unnamed child of Spellissy sadly passed away.

The most recent gunpowder explosion in the city occurred on 3 January 1837. This blast, which killed twenty people, was caused by the carelessness of one man at William Richardson's gunsmith shop on the corner of Denmark Street and O'Connell Street, which had been open for at least ten years.

On that fateful evening, some caskets of gunpowder arrived at Richardson's store. His caretaker, a man by the name of Gurde, took the delivery into the building, where he also slept. It is impossible to say how this powder ignited, as Gurde was the only person near it at the time. Perhaps he lit a candle to find his way on that dark winter's day, or a spark bounced from the room's fire. Whatever the cause, the result was sudden and drastic.

The explosion was so intense that four neighbouring houses were destroyed instantly, and twenty people were killed. The windows in the surrounding area were shattered. Even the buildings on the other side of the river felt the fury of the blast as windows of the poor house on the North Strand (now Clancy's Strand) were broken. The penetrating flash was witnessed as far away as Castleconnell.

The scene was that of desolation and ruin as a great dust cloud enveloped the area. Those in nearby buildings coughed as they made their way into the street. The walking wounded were seen trying to locate their neighbours under the rubble.

The Richardsons' housekeeper, Bridget Doolan, her husband and a neighbour, who were above the store, were killed instantly. Another occupant of the house, Robert Teskey, an apprentice, was propelled from his bed into the street, where he became one of the many injured.

Thomas McMahon's bakery had stood next door. In it was his family, a servant and a 15-year-old customer. Everyone but two of McMahon's children were killed outright. Maria Ryan, who ran a lodging house in the adjoining house, along with her three children and sister-in-law, all remarkably survived, even though many of them were buried in the rubble for several hours. Her youngest son was, like Teskey, propelled out his window, but in this case, his entire bed came with him and he landed unharmed, still in the bed, on the street. Sadly, Ryan's two servants were killed by the force of the blast.

An 1848 gunpowder token from McArdell and Bourke, gunpowder dealers of Rutland Street. (*Image courtesy of the Limerick Museum*)

Those on the street at the time were thrown in the air by the detonation. Dr John Healy and Michael O'Neill were walking nearby. The power of the explosion threw O'Neill against a wall, where he died instantly. His companion was struck by flying debris and killed outright. Rubble flew into the building on Patrick Street, some of which struck young Anne Ryan, causing her fatal injuries. Several others were removed from the rubble, only to succumb to their injuries later in hospital. These were John O'Brien, a servant at a hardware merchant on Denmark Street; Patrick Doolan of County Offaly and John Enright, a shipping pilot from Carrigaholt, who was only seven weeks married. Terence Blake survived for almost a month and was the last official death of the explosion. Bizarrely, the only living creature to survive more than a few hours in the rubble was a cat, which sprang from a cellar after three days.

In the aftermath of the explosion, the Corporation raised two proposals. First, that no gunpowder vender should have casks of more than 25lb on their premises, with only 5lb being kept on the retail floor, and any remaining kept on an upper floor. Secondly, that no gunpowder should be sold by candlelight.

As for William Richardson, it might be wondered whether he learned his lesson. It appears that he did not, as only three years later, he opened another gun manufacturing factory on Patrick Street. During an investigation to the legal limit for gunpowder in the city boundaries, an inspector entered his premises. Quickly, one of Richardson's servants absconded with a casket of gunpowder, while Richardson was found in the stable hiding two casks of gunpowder under a horse. For this flouting of the law, Richardson was fined £100 (approximately €6,000 today).

THE CLOSURE OF ST GEORGE'S CHURCH

It was important for Edmund Sexton Pery to have a religious structure for his new town. This was St George's Church, which sat on the corner of O'Connell Street and Mallow Street. The first service was held in the church on Sunday, 14 June 1789. Officiating was the Church of Ireland Bishop of Limerick, William Cecil Pery, the brother of Edmund Sexton Pery and after whom William Street, Cecil Street and Mallow Street are named. Also in attendance was Richard Maunsell Esq., Mayor of Limerick.

The church glowed by the light of a thirteenth-century stained glass window in the east wall. The window had been removed from the Franciscan Convent in St Francis's Abbey under the guidance of Lady Lucy Hartsonge. Lady Hartstonge was another of the Pery siblings. She married Henry Hartstonge, after whom Henry Street, Hartstonge Street and Sir Harry's Mall are named. The church was also lit by twelve windows in the upper gallery. This gallery was supported by six pillars.

As the Newtownpery developed and the population increased, the congregation found St George's Church too tight for comfort. The last service took place there on Sunday, 16 October 1836, when the ecclesiastical building was filled to the rafters with parishioners. The *Limerick Chronicle* wrote of the regret felt by all those in attendance.

Another member of the Maunsell family attended this last service. This time Archdeacon Maunsell officiated at the service with the assistance of Rev. Dawson Massy. As the replacement church of St Michael's in Pery Square was under construction the congregation of St George's parish attended the Wesley Methodist Chapel on Bedford Row. St Michael's church was designed by the Pain Brothers, who were responsible for many of Limerick's limestone buildings and bridges of the early nineteenth century. It took almost eight years but finally, in 1844, St Michael's Church was opened for worship.

THE GOLDEN JUBILEE OF GEORGE III

Limerick celebrated every moment of note of the reign of George III, King of Great Britain and Ireland, and these always involved pomp and ceremony. In June 1809, King George's birthday was marked with peals from the bells of St Mary's Cathedral. These were answered by salutes from the merchant vessels in the harbour. The Royal Artillery, 1st German Heavy Dragoons, 28th Regiment of Foot, Royal Tyrone and North Cork Regiments lined the streets, from the Tontine Buildings (now Pery Square) to Rutland Street, firing *feu de joie*, a formal celebratory gunfire consisting of a celebratory rifle salute. Each of the soldiers fired in succession to form a continuous sound.

Later that year, on 25 October 1809, all the shops were closed to mark the King's Golden Jubilee. This was the first day of the fiftieth year of George III's reign. A service was held in St Mary's Cathedral by the Bishop of Limerick, Charles Warburton, who travelled from England for the occasion. It was attended by Mayor Francis Lloyd and the members of the Corporation, who made their way to the cathedral in full regalia.

Once again, the streets were lined with the garrison, who fired a *feu de joie*. The city was alight with 'grand illuminations' and each street displayed images of the King. The five houses on Bank Place unfurled banners from the top of the buildings. The centre of the five houses was the image of Britannia pointing to the sun. In the centre of the sun was the word 'fifty', and in her left hand she held a scroll on which was written, 'Rejoice Britons, Britons rejoice'. Hibernia, with her harp, stood to the right of Britannia, and to the left was a Limerick scene. Those who could afford the honour attended a ball at the Assembly Rooms, held at Charlotte's Quay.

It is not surprising that Limerick celebrated the reign of George III with such spectacle, as it was during his reign that the city entered a golden age of prosperity. Not only was the Newtownpery constructed, but local merchants also reaped the rewards of the global British Empire.

THE GALLANT ELLEN O'GRADY

In 1918, Limerick-born Ellen O'Grady became the first female Deputy Police Commissioner in New York. She was born Ellen Crowley in 1865 to Timothy and Alice Crowley. She married Maurice O'Grady aged 23 and after eleven years she was left a widow with four young daughters.

She was working in the courts as a probation officer when selected for the role of police commissioner, where she oversaw six police officers. Her office had the primary duties of overseeing 'white slave traffic', crimes and offences against women and girls, social welfare and the protection of juveniles. O'Grady stayed in the role for only two years, when she quit, citing the uncooperativeness of other police commissioners while she was investigating two of their officers.

Ellen O'Grady, the first female deputy police commissioner in New York City, sitting at her desk in the New York Police Department. (*Image courtesy of Library of Congress*)

H

THE HOSPITAL IN HOSPITAL

Some people in Limerick live their entire lives in Hospital, while others leave strangers puzzled when they announce that they are going to Hospital. The bewilderment comes from a small town in the county bearing this very name. As for the hospital, it was called the Hospital of St John of Jerusalem and was founded in the early thirteenth century. It was built as a place of recovery for those making pilgrimages to the Holy Land. It later included care for the sick and provided armed escorts for those in pilgrimage. The Knights Hospitallers, an army of mounted knights, evolved from this early form of secret service.

A photograph of the interior of the ancient church in Hospital taken in 1970 with the carved memorial of a knight resting in the back left. (*Image courtesy of* Limerick Leader)

All records state that Geoffry de Marisco, the Lord Justice of Ireland, erected a church and hospital in the area. While some claim it was for the crusading Knights Hospitaller, others cite the better-known Knights Templar. Although the church is now in ruin, it contains some remarkable thirteenth-century tombs. One is said to be the tomb of Geoffry de Marisco, while the other, a double tomb, depicts a knight and his wife.

Another humorously named town is that of Effin. It was mentioned no fewer than ten times in medieval documents as Effyng, while it was Eifinn on the 1840 Ordnance Survey of Ireland. There is no concrete evidence for where this town got its name, although the sixth-century Saint Eimhin is often mentioned.

This name not only causes tourist who pass the town entry sign to giggle but was also responsible for unintentionally causing an international controversy. In 2011, residents of Effin came into conflict with the Facebook website when they could not register the town as their home. Effin was deemed by Facebook to be offensive and was blocked by the company. After a long campaign by a local resident, Ann Marie Kennedy, which was reported by both the national and international press, Facebook rescinded its policy and allowed the citizens of Effin to proudly post their home town in their profiles.

HELP! HAND GRENADE

The official motto for Limerick City is *Urbs antiqua fuit studisque asperrima belli* (an ancient city well studied in the arts of war). As a result, there are mementoes of this history dotted throughout the city. During the dredging of the Abbey River in the early 2000s several hand grenades, along with several revolvers, ammunitions and an iron mortar bomb from the 1690 siege of Limerick were recovered from the riverbed.

These were not the first, nor the last, hand grenades discovered in the city. On 21 March 1965, Robert O'Connell and Michael Kelly were carrying out building works in O'Connell's garden on Athlunkard Street. The pair were chatting as they worked until Kelly, working with a pickaxe, spotted something unusual. He picked up the egg-shaped object, which he recognised immediately. What was more shocking to the man was the missing pin.

He called for O'Connell to contact the Gardaí in Mary Street, who in turn alerted the army authorities at Sarsfield Barracks. An explosives expert, Captain Owen Tansey, was required, but he was in Cork's Collins Barracks at the time of the discovery. Tansey was rushed at high speed to Limerick, where he secured the grenade and removed it to Knockalisheen. Once there, it was detonated, causing a large crater in the ground.

Another expert made their way from Cork on 2 February 2003. This time to destroy a Mills hand grenade that was discovered earlier that day in the riverbed near Sarsfield Bridge. On 5 July 2017, yet another hand grenade was stumbled upon under Thomond Bridge. All the hand grenades found over time were dated from the 1916 to 1922 era. It is impossible to know how many more hand grenades are left to be discovered in back gardens or riverbeds of Limerick.

HECTIC HOME LIFE

The 1911 census asked the women of Ireland a very personal question: how many children they had given birth to, and how many of those children were still living. The census tells us that there were three women in Limerick that year who had given birth to twenty children.

First, Kate Blake, the youngest of these women, was 46 years old. Sadly, only ten of her children were still living at the time of the census. Of those children, five sons were still living with her and her husband John in New Street. They

Dealers stop in the middle of market day to get their photograph taken in Main Street, Abbeyfeale. (*Image courtesy of the Limerick Museum*)

were squeezed into a three-roomed house. This was a step up for the family, who ten years earlier had been living in a two-room house with six of their children and a boarder.

Next, Mary Borough and her husband Robert, who lived alone in Wolfe Tone Street in 1911, even though sixteen of their twenty children were still living. Mary was a 65-year-old grandmother at the time. Her 12-year-old granddaughter, Mary Egan, was staying with them on the night of the census. Their youngest child, Frederick Borough, was 24 at the time, the same age as their granddaughter, Theresa Carr. They too lived in a very modest home with only three rooms.

Finally, Mary Horgan from Abbeyfeale, who was fluent in both English and Irish. Only ten of her children were still living in 1911. Five of them were living with the 53-year-old and her husband, William Morris Horgan, in a small two-room thatched cottage. One of their sons, William, was an unemployed national school teacher.

I

IRETON'S ILLNESS

Henry Ireton was the son-in-law of Oliver Cromwell. Keeping it in the family, Ireton was Cromwell's man on the ground during the 1651 siege of Limerick. Limerick, as it had done during many sieges, held her ground, and it would take a year from Ireton's first arrival in Limerick for the city to surrender.

Ireton had many of the dignitaries of Limerick hanged, but it would seem karma caught up with him quickly. A plague ravished the city and Ireton fell

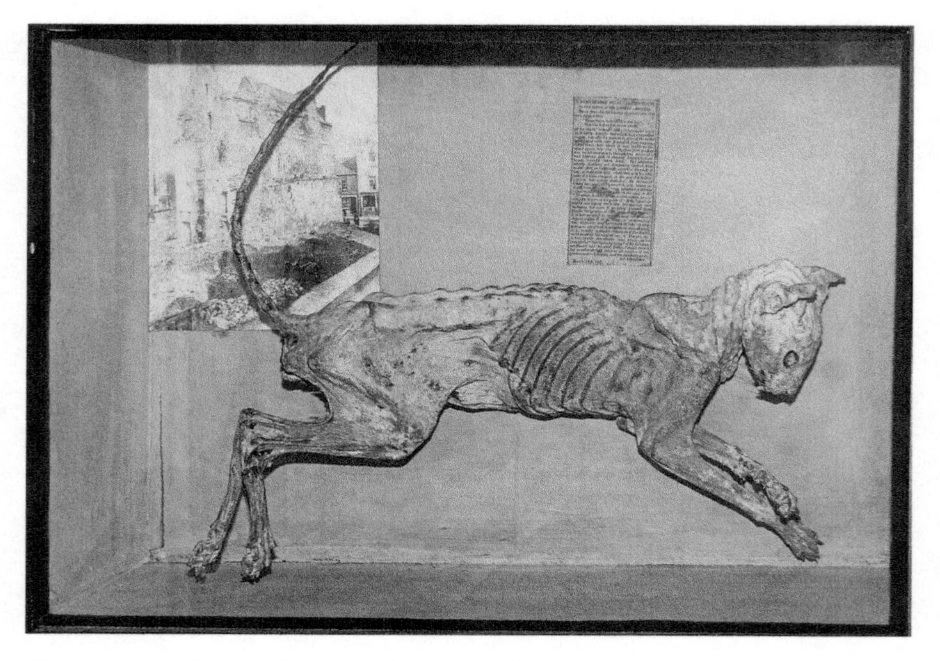

This mummified cat was discovered in the rubble of Ireton's house on Nicholas Street as it was being demolished in the 1890s. (*Image courtesy of the Limerick Museum*)

ill. Just over a month after Limerick's surrender, Ireton died from the illness in a house at the corner of Bridge Street and Nicholas Street. When the house was demolished in the 1890s, the pinnacles were moved to the grounds of St Mary's Cathedral, where they remain to this day.

Ireton's body was removed to Westminster Abbey, where it laid in peace until the restoration of the English monarchy nine years later. On 30 January 1661, Charles II had Ireton's body removed, where a posthumous execution was carried out.

A curious cat is embedded in a wall just off Roches Street. This strange creature is a stone carving of a cat with two tails. When the Casey family of Roches Street were building their poultry store in the early twentieth century, they required stones for the process. They approached a local character, Paddy Quirke, who sold them some. Among them was a carved cat with two tails. Mr Casey decided to place the stone into the facade of his building. During a later reconstruction, it was moved to the gable end, where it remains today.

One story of this curious stone tells that it was carved by the poet Carrol O'Daly, who placed it in King Donal Mor O'Brien's Palace centuries before. The palace made way for St Mary's Cathedral. When questioned, Quirke claimed that he found it in Quin Abbey, near Ennis. The second theory is more likely, as when Quirke noticed that Casey had the stone, he demanded its return. Casey instead satisfied him with a larger payment.

INCREDIBLE INVENTORS

In 1901, Denis Madden, the 20-year-old son of a lock keeper, struck on a marvellous idea. As he was raised by the water and was an oarsman who rowed with St Michaels Rowing Club, it is no surprise that his sights were set on the beautiful and majestic Shannon River. Even so, his invention would have brought with it many strange looks.

At the turn of the century, bicycles were becoming a very popular form of transport and Madden decided to combine this new trend with his passion. He set about building a boat, about 24ft long, 3ft wide and 2½ft deep. The bottom of the boat contained paddles, which were produced by the Bethell family blacksmiths. The Harrison Lee foundry created the bearings and turning axle, which was used in the manufacturing of the bicycle-like structure. Madden sat atop this structure and, using a pedalling motion, propelled the boat along the river.

This strange invention was not reserved for the bank of the river but was also tested when Madden peddled it at a rate of 8mph from Limerick to Kilrush along the body of the Shannon River. It was most certainly a sight to behold for all on the shore that day.

Madden did not hang up his inventing hat, nor his focus on the river. Five years later, he decided that there must be an easier way to cross the Shannon. For the task he created a pair of shoes that allowed him to walk on the water. One of his other more ingenious inventions was that of a device for lifting submarines from the seabed that was used by the Royal Navy.

Although he moved to Dublin a few years later, his heart was always by the water. At the time of his death in 1973, he held forty-eight lifesaving medals, the highest number granted to any one individual up to that point.

Because of a spate of fires that hit Limerick in the 1860s another inventor, William Barrington, was inspired to invent a unique type of fire escape in 1868. Barrington was a civil engineer and architect. He worked mostly on railway projects, such as the Limerick to Foynes line, but also on main drainage schemes.

His fire escape consisted of an iron balcony on the upper floors of a building. The balcony hung on pulleys that worked in a similar way to a sash window. When someone would step on to the balcony, it would descend to the ground. Once that person disembarked it would return to its position to await another passenger. He recommended to the Corporation that each house over two storeys in the city be fitted with the invention.

Another gentleman inventor was Richard Ellis, a justice of the peace in Abbeyfeale. Ellis was born about 1805 to Thomas Ellis, MP for Dublin and Dymphna Monsell of Tervoe. In 1867, he invented a new form of transport called the 'Right Carriage' that would restrain even unbroken horses and make them comply with the driver's wishes. Ellis was so keen on the invention that he sent it to be exhibited in the second world's fair, which was held in Paris. It is not known if any carriage-makers took Ellis' invention on board and developed it for general production.

J

AN UNUSUAL JUDGEMENT

In 1950, Judge Barry O'Brien sat behind his bench at Limerick Circuit Criminal Court while a young man accused of theft sat before him. The accused pleaded guilty to stealing 14st of lead from the roof of an outhouse on the North Circular Road. His excuse was that he could not find employment.

This revelation caused the judge to tell how he had only the day before given a lift to a teenager from Kildare on his way to work in a Bord na Mona site. This inspired him to implement a very unusual judgement on the proclaimed thief. He instructed the state solicitor to contact Bord na Mona to see if they had any vacancies.

The following day, the judge and the accused were back in the courtroom. Armed with the information that employment was available, he informed the young man that he could avoid conviction if he travelled to Galway to work in the bogs, with a contingency that he must pay back the £139 worth of damage he caused to the building.

Another example came about during a very strange exchange in the Limerick city police court on Tuesday, 30 December 1856. The trial was between John O'Keefe, who ran a bacon store in St Mary's Parish in the city, and an unnamed woman from Murroe.

According to John O'Keefe, the woman came into his shop and placed an order for a side of bacon, with a request for it to be cut into little pieces. Once he had completed the task, the Murroe woman changed her mind and left the shop. This left O'Keefe with 'bits and scraps upon his hands', which he would find nearly impossible to sell to another customer.

The Murroe woman attended the court with five other women from Murroe. When it became her time to speak, she brought all the women to the witness table with her for moral support. She went on to explain that she asked

O'Keefe to cut 4lb of bacon, but instead, he cut 5lb. She also stated that the piece he wanted to give her 'had no more fat on it than had a freshly polished poker'. Although he reduced the size down to 4lb, it was still far to lean for her tastes, so she left the shop, being unsatisfied with the offering.

After her testimony, O'Keefe produced the disputed meat. The magistrates looked at it and could not understand why she could object to it, as it was 'both pleasing and inviting, for it was most lusciously fat, in fact, with the exception of a few gentle streaks of lean interspersed throughout, it was a lump of fat'.

With this, the rest of the Murroe women 'commenced a kind of Dutch medley. They all spoke together – some in Irish, others in English and Irish.' The court descended into mayhem. Due to all the commotion in the court, and as O'Keefe still had his property, the magistrates decided to dismiss the case.

O'Keefe wrapped up his bacon, tucked it under his arm and left the court. He was followed by the women from Murroe, 'who kept chattering to each other in a *lingua franca*, which only themselves or the initiated could understand'. The names of the women from Murroe remain unknown to this day.

A JOURNALLED JOURNEY

By the 1850s, emigration to Australia, whether forced or voluntarily, was high on people's agendas. Those who were transported for crimes felt every hour of their journey and every day of their incarceration. The journey and slog were not much easier for those in the labouring class, emigrating for employment opportunities.

The wealthier families had a very different journey. In 1852, wealthy Limerick families were among those who voyaged down under. The families of Patrick O'Brien and Patrick Kelly took prefabricated houses with them to Australia. These could be constructed with the aid of the labourers they also took with them. Both families and the two others headed by Terence O'Brien and Edward Hogan brought their domestic servants as well. Adjusting to a new life in the island continent was not as difficult as it was for many of their fellow countrymen.

Miles Monckton, also known as Miley Muntin, a member of the landed gentry, left for Australia in 1841. He never contacted his family back in Ireland between 1845 and 1868, when he decided to take the long return journey back to Limerick.

While in Australia, his brothers, sisters and brother-in-law John W. Braddel all passed away, and he was presumed dead. His family's estate of Lisduane passed to the Braddel children. When he arrived back to his home, he was accused of being an imposter. This led to a court battle lasting five years, as Monckton attempted to receive his rightful share given to him by his father. He won his case on appeal and received £4,000.

Today it can take upwards of thirty-six hours to travel from Limerick to Brisbane, Australia, but in the mid-nineteenth century this same journey would take months. Two young Limerick men, Mark and Hamilton O'Shaughnessy, chronicled their journey for their parents, Mark Terry O'Shaugnessy and Jane Massy, who ran a coach and carriage agency in Catherine Street.

In 1859, both brothers enlisted in the Royal Irish Constabulary. Hamilton was both the elder and taller of the pair at 21 years old and 6ft tall. Mark was behind him by two years and two inches.

Four years later, when the opportunity arose for members of the constabulary to act as guards on the long journey southwards the brothers signed up quickly. They boarded the *Beejauore* at Queenstown, now Cobh, in County Cork on 23 March 1863. Their duty quickly began, as when the ship was leaving port four stowaways were discovered. They were quickly returned to shore with a clergyman. On another note, it was reported from the same vessel that one Mrs Brown was left husbandless, as he had departed the ship and failed to return before the anchor was lifted.

The ship sailed for six days before reaching the coast of Spain. Here, one of the sailors caught a small shark, much to the delight of the passengers. As they sailed past the Tropic of Cancer on 5 April 1863, the passengers began to get cabin fever. Constables were put on duty to prevent the young women and men interacting after lights out at ten o'clock at night. The mingling came to a head on 12 April, when the priest on board warned the girls that he would not write them a good reference if they continued interacting with the boys. Later in the journey, some of the girls would dress in male clothing and pass themselves off as men to avoid the curfew.

Over the ensuing days, many of the passengers took to sleeping on deck as the heat below deck was stifling. The passengers even began showing signs of scabies and scurvy. Every few days they would pass a ship returning to the northern hemisphere, where letters and newspapers were exchanged. Their journey took them by the coast of Brazil. Here, on 28 April, both sailors and passengers took the opportunity to swim in the sea.

On May Day, a fight broke out between the Irish and the English. This became a common occurrence. On board there were 300 passengers from Lancashire, who had free passage, twenty from Scotland and the rest were all Irish.

On 17 May, the ship finally rounded the Cape and made it into the Pacific Ocean; with this the temperature changed drastically, too. Some of the passengers remained in their bed all day due to the rough sea and cold weather. The ship was tossed back and forth for the next two weeks. The crew and passengers were surprised, and dismayed, when by 2 June, the deck was covered in snow.

Theft was common on board and on 26 May, a man from London attempted to steal the O'Shaughnessys' bacon from their room. Mark did mention that if it were not for the provisions they brought themselves they would be half starved. He noted that there was nowhere near enough provisions on the ship for all the passengers.

As they neared the coast of Tasmania on 11 June, the captain gave the girls, much to their delight, two bottles of wine. As a protective measure, the door to their cabin was locked to prevent male intruders. Four days later, they met a ship coming from Rockhampton, the first stop on the Australian coast. The next stop was on 24 June, at Port Curtis. Here many other passengers boarded a steamer for Rockhampton, while others waited to go to Brisbane.

During the journey there were thirty-seven deaths, only four of those being adults. These were a father of six called Dwyer from Tipperary, a young man called Collins from Kerry who was only married for four months, a woman known only as Mrs Gillespie, and the last of the four was sadly a roommate of the O'Shaughnessy brothers. He was 20-year-old Robert Campion from Kilkenny. He was on deck smoking when he was hit by the flapping sail, which tossed him overboard. Campion left his younger sister behind him.

It wasn't all itching, scratching, fighting and death. The O'Shaughnessy brothers also mentioned singing and dancing that took place all over the ship, stating there was a family of Irish flute players that were the best Mark had ever heard. There were also ten children born during the trip.

The O'Shaughnessy brothers travelled to Brisbane first but found it to be a small town without much activity, even though they were pleased that the Australian winters were warmer than the Irish summers. They soon moved to Sydney, where three years later Hamilton married Irish woman Kate Brennan. The brothers were soon joined by their sister, Ellen O'Shaughnessy.

A JAPANESE EDUCATION

In 1890, Mary Angela Fitzgerald was born in Galbally as the eldest daughter of two school teachers. She was sadly orphaned before her fifteenth birthday. Luckily, her spinster aunt returned from Canada to raise Fitzgerald and her six siblings. She followed in her parents' footsteps, qualifying as a school teacher when aged 20. She joined the Infant Jesus Sisters at the Drishane Convent on Millstreet in Cork.

Tragedy seemed to follow the Sister. In 1919, she went on a mission to Japan. Here she taught English and piano to the poor in Yokohama, about 30km from Tokyo. On 1 September 1923, the convent and surrounding area were destroyed by an earthquake. Sister Angela was attending mass that morning when the roof of the church collapsed. She was the sole survivor of the 246 people inside.

Despite this, and most likely because of it, Sister Angela remained in the area to help rebuild the community. Her talent for teaching English was well renowned. In 1938, a local businessman, Hidesaburō Shōda, requested that Sister Angela taught his daughter, Michiko. It was not known at the time that this 5-year-old girl was destined for a very interesting life.

Sadly, Sister Angela was interred as a prisoner of war in Japan in 1942, as she held a British passport. It would take two years and interference from the Irish government for Sister Angela, and twelve other Irish nuns, to be released. This did not deter her from her mission, remaining in Japan and continuing to teach without missing a beat. She visited Ireland only twice in all those years, once in 1946 and again in 1973. After her death in 1980, she was buried in the Infant Jesus cemetery in Japan.

As for her young English student. In 1957, Michiko met Crown Prince Akihito while playing tennis. A romance blossomed between the pair and they were married two years later, when she became the Crown Princess of Japan. Upon the death of her father-in-law Emperor Shōwa on 7 January 1989, her husband became Emperor of Japan and she Empress. When she visited Ireland in 2005, she recalled the education she received from Irish nuns.

JUDGES' DECREES

The year famine broke out in Ireland the local courts found themselves very busy. The day 15 March 1844, saw the following cases brought before the Limerick City Petty Sessions. For the heinous crime of cutting Christopher

Delmege's hedges in Castlepark, Michael Doyle and his assistant had the choice to pay a fine of £2 or spend two months in prison.

A warrant for information was ordered against Jane O'Connor, who was described in the court as 'a lady of pleasure' after she was accused of stealing a sailor's jacket. More information was also required by the judge in the case of Michael M'Iniery versus James Fitzgerald. M'Iniery accused Fitzgerald of stealing his donkey.

The more serious cases were heard at the County Assize that same day. These saw eight men transported to Australia for periods ranging from seven years to life. Their crimes included one for assault on a person, one for assault on a house, two for 'violation of a person' and the remaining four for highway robbery. Two men, Patrick Lynch and Edmond Conway, were sentenced to death by hanging for the murder of Rev. Charles Dawson.

Of those sentenced to between twelve months and two years' imprisonment, twelve were men. Bridget Molony, who had been found guilty of sheep stealing, was the lone woman. The two lesser sentences read that day were six months for Ellen Kennedy for the abandonment of her infant and two months for Bridget Buckley for theft.

BEWARE OF JAWS

When taps were turned on throughout the city in 1892, the locals were hit with a bizarre surprise. The new piping system laid out by Mr Dixon, at the exorbitant cost of £35,000, consisted of pipes that went directly from the river to the kitchens of the residents. The pipes turned out to be a perfect size for wriggly eels looking for a new home. As a result, the snakelike fish made their way into the city, and into the kitchens of many unsuspecting homes. The problem was quickly resolved by adding grating over the intake pipes.

Eels were a common dish on the tables in Limerick. They were usually boiled in milk before being served. However, the majority of eels caught in the Shannon River were exported to the markets of London, where they ended up as jellied eels.

Another interesting water creature made its way into the city in 1826. A young shark swam up the tidal Shannon to the quays, where it became stranded. It was an unusual sight in the city and as such it was taken to the home of George O'Connell at 116 O'Connell Street, where it was put on display for the residents of the area.

The boats of the Strand fishermen waiting for their occupants to head towards the Shannon Estuary. (*Image courtesy of Steve Ludlow*)

K

KILLED AT KILMALLOCK

In 1992, Pope John Paul II beatified Bishop Patrick O'Hely and Fr Conn O'Rourke. The pair were martyred when they refused to denounce their faith, even on the threat of death.

Limerick was in a state of hostility during the 1570s, as the House of Desmond was divided. The religious men landed in Dingle after sailing from Brittany. O'Rourke was the son of the wealthy Lord of West Breifne (now County Leitrim). The men made their way to Desmond Castle at Askeaton. Here, while the Earl was away, they were entertained by his wife, Eleanor of Desmond.

Ruins of the Dominican Abbey in Kilmallock. The Abbey founded in 1291 and was sacked by Cromwellian forces in 1648. (*Author's collection*)

Although they sought refuge with the Desmonds, they were betrayed by Eleanor as they left for Limerick. Three days later they were seized by the Mayor of Limerick, who placed them in the hands of Lord Justice William Drury. Drury tortured them to discover if the pope and King Philip II of Spain had plans for invading Ireland and to get them to renounce their faith. The pair did not relent. In August 1579, they were hanged, and their bodies remained suspended from the gallows for fourteen days in Kilmallock. Their crime: refusing to swear an oath of supremacy and acknowledge Queen Elizabeth I as the head of the church.

KURT RUSSELL

In the summer of 1968, the Disney movie studio arrived in Ireland to spend nine weeks filming *Guns in the Heather* in a location in Co. Clare. Among the cast was a young upcoming actor named Kurt Russell. To get into his character as an American exchange student in Ireland, Russell had to learn to play hurling. He described the sport as a 'weird combination of baseball and hockey', but also called it 'tough but fun'. It took him some time to master bouncing the sliotar on the hurl.

While in Ireland, Russell and his fellow actors spent a great deal of time and money in the Limerick region. One August night that summer, the then 17-year-old Russell with his fellow actors, along with sports stars Denis Law, Nobby Stiles and Bobby Charlton, arrived at the greyhound track in Markets Field for a fun night out with the dogs. During the show, Russell was asked to lead out Ned Quinlivan's hound, Broadford Toast. He received rapturous applause as he paraded around in a white coat. To his delight, Russell had led out the winner of that evening's race.

Guns in the Heather had its Limerick premiere at the Savoy Cinema in July 1970. It was part of a double feature by Disney. The other movie that evening was *One Hundred and One Dalmatians.*

DR KENNETH KAUNDA

Limerick has a unique connection with the first president of Zambia through Fr Robert Thompson, a native of Mallow. Thompson spent eleven years in Zambia, formerly Northern Rhodesia, before returning to Limerick. While

Dr Kenneth Kaunda, President of Zambia receiving the Freedom of Limerick in 1964. (*Image courtesy of* Limerick Leader)

in Zambia he befriended Dr Kenneth Kaunda. On 18 May 1963, Kaunda visited Limerick for the first time after accepting an invite from Thompson, who was involved with Crescent College at the time. Kaunda spent the night in the home of Thomas E O'Donnell, on the Ennis Road.

The following year, Kaunda became the first president of independent Zambia. Two weeks later, he returned to Limerick, this time to receive the Freedom of the City. On the day of honour, crowds gathered along the Ennis Road towards the city to try and catch a glimpse of the president. The mass of people grew so large that Gardai Special Forces were on duty at the junction of Sarsfield Street and O'Connell Street to control the crowd. It was at this location the president's car came to a stop, causing the crowd to explode into cheers.

Curiously, the honour was being performed at the School of Music on Mulgrave Street, instead of the Town Hall in Rutland Street. This was to facilitate the numbers of those in attendance. The Zambian National Anthem was played as the new president made his way to the stand. The enormous crowd remained perfectly silent as he received the Freedom of the City, after which they erupted in applause. Kaunda ended his speech by thanking the crowd in Irish, 'Go raibh maith agaibh go leir agus go mairidh sibh slan.'

President Kaunda was the forty-third Freeman of Limerick. The forty-second person to receive the honour was John F. Kennedy, president of the United States of America. Kaunda was the longest-running president of Zambia, holding office for twenty-seven years. After 1972, he changed the country to a one-party state. He was finally deposed in 1991 and a multi-party government was reinstated.

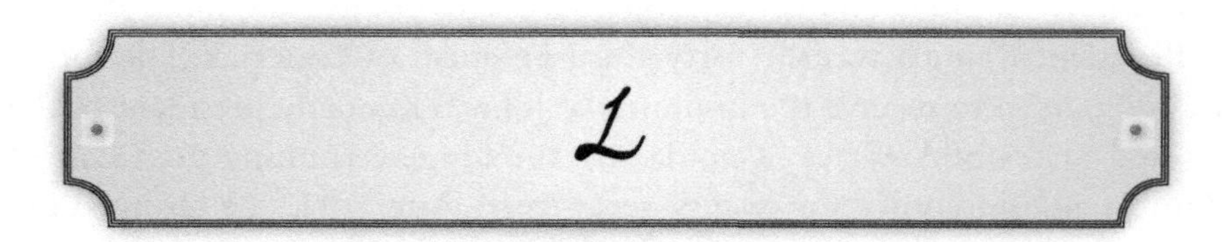

LIGHTNING LIGHTS LAST

Today we know the dangers of lightning and have regulations in place, so buildings are fitted with lightning rods and flame-retardant roofs. This was, of course, not always the case, in the times when thatched cottages were popular both in the city and county. These roof constructions not only provided grounding for the lightning, but also fuel for the resulting spark.

A traditional thatched cottage in county Limerick in the 1930s. (*Image courtesy of the Limerick Museum*)

One of the most violent lightning storms struck Limerick at half-past seven on Sunday evening, 22 July 1827. The oldest inhabitants of the city could not recall one as intense. The storm began with an extremely hot and sultry atmosphere, the clouds hanging low and heavy. Then lightning burst forth accompanied by heavy rain, closely followed by a distant roll of thunder. The flashes of lightning were so bright they illuminated the horizon, exposing at intervals the moon and stars twinkling in curious form through the dense clouds.

The lightning struck the thatched roof of Mr Dundon's house at Annaholty, near Castleconnell. It smashed the windows of the cottage and set the entire building ablaze. Outside the cottage, some milkmaids were also struck, and they were found lying prostrate on the ground with their milk pails scattered about them.

The destruction of this storm was felt not only in Limerick but also in surrounding counties of Clare and Tipperary, with several individuals losing their lives and immeasurable property damage left in the wake of the storm.

LAST CASE OF LEPROSY

The last case of leprosy possibly took place in Limerick in January 1864. It was the first case of leprosy in Ireland in thirty years. The unfortunate victim was 23-year-old Mary Hurley, who worked as a laundress for sailors in the docks. It was presumed that she encountered this ancient disease while scrubbing an infected article of clothing.

She became ill, but given her position in society and her presumed lack of funds she waited a month before seeking medical attention. She was moved quickly to the County Infirmary, now the Limerick College of Further Education on Mulgrave Street. The medical staff who attended her all wore face masks to avoid contamination. She was a medical marvel in the city as not one of the doctors in the city had seen the disease outside of a medical textbook. Sadly, there was no cure and Hurley passed away within a few weeks of entering the hospital. Fortunately, no one who came in contact with the young woman became infected.

LOSS OF A LIBRARY

A library is much more than a collection of books, it is an insight into the past, present and future. It is a container for the human experience and a meeting place for a community. The loss of a library can be extremely traumatic for a community.

On the morning of 22 February 1944, a fire raged through three buildings in the heart of the city. The fire began in a store owned by Messrs Sutton and quickly swept in through the back of the Limerick County Library. As would be expected, the books provided excellent kindling and the fire travelled unhindered through the building. The inferno ate through the entire library collection of 9,000 books.

A few weeks later an appeal was posted to the public asking for book donations to restock the shelves. The donations came swiftly, as the citizens gave publications from every genre. This created the building blocks for the new library, which became a very popular library with thousands of books from the public, for the public.

LLOYD'S LAWS

The mayors in days of yore had a lot more power and responsibility than they do in Ireland today. In October 1809, Francis Lloyd was both the mayor and chief magistrate of Limerick. During that month he enacted several by-laws. One was to regulate the weights and measures of milk cans.

Another was aimed at keeping the streets clean. He declared that street sweepers must begin their day at seven in the morning. This was also the cut-off time for households to throw their waste into the streets. The households would instead have to wait to hear the bell of a scavenger cart to dispose of their waste. With these rulings he expected the streets to be spotless by ten o'clock each morning. Along this same vein, he announced that the owners of stray pigs would be fined 5*s*.

It was quite common for families in the Englishtown to keep a pig in their houses or back garden. Pigs could be dangerous. In 1788, a young child, who was left unattended in a house in Flag Lane, was killed by the household swine. Another of Lloyd's ways to keep the streets clean in the morning was to forbid public houses from staying open past eleven o'clock at night or from opening at all on a Sunday.

Although many of Lloyd's rulings were positive, some would be looked at with a quizzical eye today. While carrying out his duties, he seized several carcases of spoiled meat from the market. His plan was not to destroy this meat but instead to have it sent to the poor inhabitants of the 'House of Industry' and 'Hospital for Lunatics' for dinner.

M

MANCHESTER MARTYRS

On 11 September 1867, two prominent Fenians, Colonel Thomas Kelly and Captain Timothy Deasy, were arrested in the centre of Manchester on a vagrancy charge. Seven days later, the two prisoners were taken from the court house in Manchester to the county jail in Hyde Road in West Gorton.

On the journey, the van was seized by about thirty men. The police offered little resistance and quickly fled. The rescuers first tried to open the van from the outside, but all these attempts failed. They called upon Police Sergeant Brett, who was inside the van, to open the door. Sergeant Brett put his eye to the keyhole as a shot was fired at the lock, killing him immediately. After a chase, the police made twenty-nine arrests. By November five of the men arrested for taking part in the rescue were found guilty and sentenced to death.

Of those five, three were publicly hanged on 23 November 1867, while the other two escaped execution. On Sunday, 8 December 1867, the citizens of Limerick held a mock funeral for the executed men. It was organised by the local trade unions and Fenians. A parade began at the Mechanics Institute on Bank Place. It continued through the city to Wolfe Tone Street, returning through the city. The procession crossed Baal's Bridge up through the Englishtown before crossing at Thomond Bridge. The crowd passed the Treaty Stone, which was covered and decorated with rosettes and shamrocks. They continued to Sarsfield Bridge and up William Street to Mount Saint Lawrence Cemetery.

A hearse pulled by six horses, wearing the traditional funeral dress, headed the procession. Girls could then be seen marching six abreast, wearing green veils, green ribbons and green rosettes with mourning centres. Next came a procession of boys, including one hundred members of the Catholic Young Men's Society and the Boherbuoy brass band playing Handel's Death March.

Afterwards, the trades of the city, including coopers, masons, tobacconists, tailors, painters, bootmakers, carpenters, plasterers, bootmakers, bakers, cork-cutters, victuallers, fishermen and many others marched through the streets. Finally, the Englishtown fife and drum band, along with hundreds of people from the countryside, concluded this procession.

Once the 'funeral' reached the cemetery, Father Quaid of O'Callaghan's Mills, Co. Clare, prayed for the souls of the three executed men, after which the crowd dispersed in peace. The parade was immense and although the police did not interfere with the demonstration, they did identify and name 437 individuals of importance as having attended.

Twenty years later, on 9 December 1887, the memorial in Mount Saint Lawrence Cemetery was unveiled amid controversy. The planned unveiling was Sunday, 27 November 1887, after the government issued a statement that the military and police would surround the cemetery and disperse any persons that ventured to assemble there.

The memorial was due to be unveiled by Dr John McInerney, a native of Limerick and a prominent Nationalist who had arrived in Limerick a day earlier. McInerney was greeted at the train station by a large crowd, which was quickly dispersed by the police. McInerney attempted to address the crowd once more when he reached his hotel. Once again, the rowdy audience had to be broken up by the police. Approximately thirty people were admitted to Barrington's Hospital due to the injuries they received from police batons.

The day of the unveiling arrived and as promised the memorial was surrounded by military, turning away all spectators, who left despondent but not defeated. A few days later, following the death of Edward Hartney, a prominent Nationalist, a plan was hatched. The committee would use Hartney's funeral as a decoy to unveil the memorial. This passed with relative ease as the police who were in attendance that day made no effort to disperse the crowd; instead, they made note of the attendees.

A MAYORAL MUDDLE

In 2014, the Limerick City Council and the Limerick County Council merged. As a result, there was a doubling of many of the roles within the council. This included the highest office of both, the mayor in the city and the Cathaoirleach in the county. The role of mayor had existed in the city since the twelfth century, while the Cathaoirleach had been in place since 1898.

Statue of Patrick Walsh in front of The Old Union Station, Augusta, Georgia, USA. (*Image courtesy of George Lane*)

After the merger, the Cathaoirleach was considered the higher role, encompassing both the city and county; while the role of mayor remained in place only for the metropolitan district of the city. The information about this role was not well known outside of the county area. This led to the first new Cathaoirleach to ask for the role name to be changed to that of Mayor of Limerick City and County. If that was not confusing enough, both of the mayors of Limerick in 2014 had the surname Sheehan and were also from from Askeaton.

In 2019, the role of the mayor of the metropolitan district was renamed the Cathaoirleach. While the former role of Cathaoirleach was to be the only mayor in town. To add even more confusion to the matter, in 2019, it was decided in a public vote that Limerick was to have a directly elected mayor for the first time. This was to replace the role of CEO of the Limerick City and County Council, who is currently neither the mayor nor the Cathaoirleach.

Another aspect of mayoral interest comes from Limerick citizens who would go on to become mayors of other cities. Rathkeale man William Fitzgibbon became the Lord Mayor of Cork in 1856 and 1857. Fitzgibbon first arrived in Cork to open a business on Shandon Street and within a few short years he had expanded to Washington Street. In 1850, he created a department store in Grand Parade. His genius in business soon led him into politics, where he was appointed as mayor. Interestingly, he donated his entire mayoral salary to charitable institutions. A Limerick woman, Kathleen Clarke, was also the first female Lord Mayor of Dublin from 1939 to 1941.

Meanwhile, further afield, Ballylanders born John T. Browne, became the mayor of Houston, Texas, between 1892 and 1896. Patrick Walsh was born in Ballingarry in 1840 but left Limerick twelve years later with his family for Charleston, South Carolina. He rose through the newspaper ranks before entering politics in 1870, becoming a senator in 1894. He was not re-elected to the post and instead became the Mayor of Augusta, Georgia, in 1897. He passed away suddenly only two years later. In 1913, a statue was raised in his honour in Augusta.

McDONNELL'S MARGARINE

When William McDonnell was born in 1835 as one of twelve children of an affluent family, no one could have predicted the impact he would have on Irish cuisine. As a young man, William was an all-round athlete and swimmer. He was known as a fine baritone singer and was frequently heard at local concerts. He served as a Limerick City treasurer, member of the Limerick Harbour Board and the President of Chamber of Commerce. Following his father Thaddeus McDonnell's death in 1871, McDonnell entered into a partnership with his brother, Charles, under the name of W. & C. McDonnell, producing dairy products.

In 1869, margarine was invented by the French chemist Hippolyte Mège-Mouriès and William was fascinated by this cheaper substitute for butter. He went to visit the chemist and after he learned the production process he returned to Limerick. Finally, in 1876 he opened the first factory in Ireland. By 1880, the factory moved to Thomas Street, where it became the first factory in the world to manufacture margarine on a mass scale.

In 1912, the factory was moved to Waterford City to be closer to its British and Continental customers and then in 1951 to Drogheda, where the firm opened the world's most modern margarine factory. The firm's products included Summer County margarine, Blue Band margarine, Flora, Cookeen, Calve oil, Tree Top orange squash, and Royco soups. W. & C. McDonnell's was taken over by the Campbell Soup Company in the late 1990s and the Drogheda factory closed in 2003.

MIXED UP MATRIMONY

The road of love is not always a smooth one, especially when couples must contend with some of the strange laws that were once on the books in Ireland. Bridget O'Connell, along with Patrick and Michael Hartigan, of Pennywell, became the centre of a scandal after she fell for the two brothers.

On 24 February 1900, Rev. Matthew McNamara at Castleconnell Catholic Church performed the wedding of 20-year-old Bridget O'Connell, of Lisnagry to Patrick Hartigan, of Pennywell. Patrick was seven years older than her at the time of matrimony.

The couple moved to Pennywell and started a family. Tragically, Patrick passed away following a short illness on 23 March 1907, leaving Bridget to raise their four living children. Bridget remained in contact with her in-laws, especially her brother-in-law, Michael. Michael, as he tended to the needs of his nephews and nieces, formed a special bond with Bridget, one that ultimately evolved into love.

In May 1909, the pair wished to have their relationship recognised, so they went to St John's Cathedral and they asked for dispensation to be married. Fr A. Murphy refused the couple because the marriage contravened the law that stipulated a widow could not marry her deceased husband's brother. This law had recently been repealed in England as part of the 'Deceased Wife's Sister's Marriage Act 1907' but it was still illegal in Ireland and would remain so until 1914. Fr Murphy believed that only the Pope could issue a dispensation for the marriage to take place and although he had heard of cases of a widower marrying his deceased wife's sister, he never heard a case where a widow wished to marry her deceased husband's brother.

Undaunted, on 1 November 1909, Bridget, Michael and another woman went to see Fr P. McInerney, the new parish priest in Castleconnell, to apply to be married. The marriage took place just over two weeks later in Castleconnell.

Unfortunately, a series of clerical errors foiled their chances at a happily ever after. Fr McInerney had recorded the incorrect date of marriage, as well as making errors in the names of the bride and both fathers of the couple. As he was new to the parish, Fr McInerney went to St John's Cathedral for advice, whereupon he spoke to Fr Murphy and the truth was uncovered.

The couple were summoned to the Castleconnell Petty Sessions twice in 1910 for making false statements on the Register of Marriages for the Registrar's District of Annacotty, County Limerick. The couple were found guilty and punished by having their marriage annulled. During the intervening

The main street of Castleconnell in the early 1900s. (*Image courtesy of Limerick Museum*)

months, Bridget had become pregnant. When their son, Thomas Hartigan, was born in June 1910 the pair were no longer officially married. Sadly, the baby would not survive infancy and was buried in the same grave as his uncle in Mount Saint Lawrence Cemetery.

After the scandal and her great loss, Bridget returned to her mother's home in Lisnagry. During the census of 1911, Bridget was recorded as a widow. Meanwhile, Michael Hartigan was also living with his parents, but he was recorded as married with the stipulation 'wife living in County Limerick' on his census return.

n

NORWEGIAN IMMIGRANTS

In May 1868, Limerick became home to some surprising visitors from Norway. Unlike their ancient ancestors, the Vikings, these newer arrivals sought refuge in the city. On 12 April 1868, the *Hannah Parr* set sail from Christiania (now Oslo), Norway, bound for Quebec, Canada. The ship was carrying 366 emigrants – with ages ranged from those born on the journey to a 74-year-old – and crew on a voyage due to take fifty-one days. Their journey took an unexpected turn after two weeks at sea and it was to be 107 days before her passengers were disembarked in America.

Once the ship hit the Atlantic it was struck by an intense storm, which caused extreme damage to the mast and steering devices. Within a few days, the crew had strapped a sail together and plotted a course for the nearest port for repairs. That port was Limerick. They arrived in the city on 7 May 1868, after spending the previous day at Scattery.

The ship was towed into the floating docks on Thursday night for refitting. Every provision was made for their comfort by the Norwegian consul, Mr M.R. Ryan, who had visited them and seen after their wants. The ship was moored at one of Richard Russell's docking sheds for repairs by Messrs Ryan, Brothers, & Co.

Sadly, the Norwegians' stay was not entirely pleasant, as several young children died while the ship was docked in Limerick. Infant mortality was high, so some death was not entirely surprising. The children who passed away were all buried in St Munchin's churchyard. In 2008, the Limerick Civic Trust raised a plaque in the churchyard near the grave of Anne Kearse in their memory.

While the Norwegians waited in Limerick, great efforts were made to keep them entertained. A city woman, 48-year-old Anne Kearse, was instrumental in helping them by writing to the press asking the public for contributions of money, food and clothing.

The migrants spent one of the evenings in the Protestant Orphan Hall, Baker's Place, listening to the inmates of the 'female Blind Asylum', Catherine Street, singing hymns. The tables in the hall were decorated with seasonal flowers.

While the ship was being repaired, the passengers slept in a docking shed, returning to the ship when it was safe to do so. Finally, on 9 June 1868, at about eight o'clock in the morning *Hannah Parr* departed from Limerick. An enormous crowd of local citizens had gathered to wave goodbye.

Prior to the vessel leaving the dock, one old man, as he was boarding the ship with tears in his eyes, turned to the ladies and gentlemen whom he had just shaken hands with, took out a pocket book, opened it and handed it, along with a pencil, to one of the gentleman, at the same time pointing to a blank leaf, motioning for him to write something in it as a souvenir; so the gentleman took the book and immediately wrote in it the following sentence: 'God bless the *Hannah Parr* with her living freight, and bring them through a speedy and prosperous voyage to the land of their adoption; and bless them abundantly for time and eternity.' The old man next presented the book to another gentleman, who wrote in it, 'with feelings of deep regret, both I and my family part with our dear Norwegian friends'.

The Docks where the Hannah Parr was repaired. (*Image courtesy of Steve Ludlow*)

The Limerick branch of the Hibernian Bible Society gave 154 copies of the Bible, in Danish and Norwegian, to the stranded emigrants.

The *Hannah Parr* was towed by two steamers, the *Privateer* and *Bulldog*, to Foynes, where it remained for a few days before continuing the voyage to Quebec. She arrived in her destination port on 28 July 1868. It would take until 15 August before news of her safe arrival was reported in Limerick. The following month, a letter was received in Limerick from the captain of the *Hannah Parr* thanking the citizens of the city for their kindness and hospitality.

The same storm that hit the *Hannah Parr* was disastrous to many other ships, including the *Eloise*, which was owned by John McDonnell and Sons, of Limerick. The ship had left Limerick in April with ballast to Quebec, and on its return journey with timber it was sunk by the storm. Similarly, the *Raudier*, of Sunderland, had left Limerick about the same time as the *Eloise* bound for Montreal and floundered while returning with a shipment of grain.

NIXON

The visit of the American President John F. Kennedy to Limerick in 1963, is not only remembered by the citizens but is also honoured through street and school names. What is not as well known is that another American President visited the city seven years later.

On 3 October 1970, President Richard Milhous Nixon and the first lady Pat Nixon nee Ryan, landed at Shannon Airport. He was on a three-day tour of Ireland. The President was greeted by the Taoiseach, Jack Lynch, and Dr Patrick Hillary, Minister of External Affairs. Soon the cavalcade was en route to Limerick.

As they passed the Greenhills Hotel, Ennis Road, the President noticed a wedding couple watching the cars pass. Nixon stopped his car, presented the new bride with some of the flowers he had received, shook the groom's hand and wished him luck. There were over 800 Gardai in the city that day, and they ate 280 loaves of bread along with the tea and soup provided by Myles Breen.

The visit came at the height of the Vietnam War and this resulted in several protests, including Councillor Joe Quinn, whose placard was torn up by fellow councillor Alderman Stephen Coughlan. Other protesters included the Trade Unionist and Labour party member Jim Kemmy, who had his placard pulled from him by the Gardai.

The Nixons with members of the Limerick Council on arriving in the city, where gifts were exchanged. One of the gifts, given by Mayor Liddy, was a blackthorn stick. Alderman Coughlan turned to Mrs Nixon and remarked: 'Now you'll have something to beat him with if he gets out of line.'

Once the official duties were completed, the Nixons travelled to Kilfrush House in Knocklong, where they were welcomed by over 200 people outside the gate. Nixon left the car and walked through the crowd, shaking hands and greeting people. At the time Kilrush House was owned by Irish-born, New York-based millionaire John A. Mulcahy. That night dinner included Irish lamb stew and Irish wood pigeon, served by the staff of Hanratty's Hotel, while flowers came from the Flower Studio in Cecil Street.

Others in the White House entourage were the national security adviser, Henry Kissinger, and Chief of Staff Bob Haldeman, who was later imprisoned for his role in the Watergate scandal. Also staying in Limerick for this visit were over 200 members of the international press, all clamouring to get a quote from the President.

Limerick was also visited by President Bill Clinton and the first lady Hillary Clinton on a sunny September day in 1998. A platform was raised on O'Connell Street for the event and 40,000 people lined the streets to catch a glimpse of the couple. President Clinton received the Freedom of Limerick from Mayor Joe Harrington and the couple rested for the night in Adare Manor.

NEWCASTLE WEST TO NEW YORK

John Wolfe Ambrose was born in Newcastle West in 1838 but when he was 14 years old his family relocated to New York. As a young man, Ambrose attended Princeton University and after graduating he flitted between several occupations before settling into a role in construction.

His company's primary work involved building elevated roads and laying piping, although he was also involved in the construction of private buildings. His most notable work was on the New York harbour, which improved the viability of the Port of New York, contributing to making New York City the heart of commerce in the United States.

A channel and ship were named in his honour a year after his death in 1899. Then, over thirty-five years after his passing, a monument was erected in his honour in Battery Park, New York City. On 15 May 2018, the monument was rededicated in a ceremony attended by numerous of Ambrose's descendants. The

Ambrose Channel remains the main entrance to New York from the Atlantic Ocean to this day.

In 1936, a memorial to John Wolfe Ambrose was unveiled in Battery Park, New York City, by Mayor Fiorello La Guardia. In 1990, the bust was stolen from the memorial, it took until 2017 for the bust to be replaced. (*Image courtesy of the New York City Parks Department*)

Another Limerick man literally held back the current in California with his engineering prowess. Michael O'Shaughnessy was born on 28 May 1864 in Loughill. In 1884, he graduated with a degree in engineering from the Royal University of Dublin. He left Ireland for San Francisco, California, with his degree in hand the following year.

His skills were in high demand on the rugged west coast of America. He was soon planning railroad systems, including the famous tram system that is still in use today. From 1889, O'Shaughnessy oversaw water supply projects on the Hawaiian Islands, which developed his skills in water transportation.

In 1912, he became the chief engineer for San Francisco. He was tasked with bringing clean fresh water to San Francisco through the Hetch Hetchy Reservoir. The project began in 1914 and used a system of dams and tunnels to carry water over 250km from Yosemite to the city. O'Shaughnessy was the lead on the project until the San Francisco Public Utilities Commission was formed in 1932. The reservoir opened on 28 October 1934 but tragically O'Shaughnessy passed away only sixteen days earlier. The Hetch Hetchy Dam was renamed the O'Shaughnessy Dam in his honour.

One of the most unusual occupations held by a Limerick man would be that of Martin 'Mart' Duggan, who made a name for himself as a gunslinger in the Wild West. Duggan was born in Limerick on 10 November 1848. Like so many others from that period in Irish history, he left Ireland to go to New York with his family when he was a young boy. When he was only 15 years old he set out west.

Duggan worked his way through mining towns, building up a reputation as a strong man. In 1876, he was hired as bouncer in a saloon in Georgetown, Colorado. He was very quickly involved in his first gunfight after being threatened by a drunken patron at the saloon. The pair faced off on the street and Duggan's bullets struck first.

Two years later he was appointed as marshal in the aptly named Leadville, Colorado. While on duty, he protected a murder suspect from being lynched because of his race. The suspect was later acquitted. He brought widespread peace to the area during his two years in office but left after a series of disagreements with the wealthier members of the town. However, he later returned to a role of patrol man in Leadville in 1887. In the early morning of 9 April 1888, Duggan had an argument with two gamblers and challenged them to come outside to settle the disagreement in a duel. Knowing his reputation, they both refused. As he was leaving for home, he was approached from behind and shot in the back. He died later that day from his wounds, but it was never discovered who pulled the trigger.

NAISH THE NATURAL

In 1896, J. Carrol Naish was born Joseph Patrick Carroll Naish in New York. He was the son of Patrick Sarsfield Naish of Ballycullen House, Askeaton, and Catherine Moran of Foynes. Although his parents lived only a few miles apart in Ireland, they first met in New York.

J. Carrol's talent for acting was appreciated by those around him from a young age. He joined the Gus Edwards' vaudeville troupe as a child. Previous members of this troupe included the famous Marx Brothers. The outbreak of the First World War put an end to his acting for a period, as he enlisted in the US Army Signal Corps.

When the war came to an end, Carrol remained in Paris for a few years working as a singer and dancer. In 1926, he returned to the United States, this time to California, where he made his first appearance on screen in the silent movie *What Price Glory*. He was typecast as a villain in most of his 225 television roles and film appearances. In 1943 he played Dr Daka, Batman's first on-screen nemesis.

In 1943, he received an Academy Award nomination for his supporting role in *Sahara*. He was nominated for an Academy Award again in 1945 for *A Medal for Benny*, a role for which he received a Golden Globe. He is honoured with a star on the Hollywood Walk of Fame.

J. Carrol returned to Limerick in 1957 to visit the birthplaces of both his parents. He sojourned in Cruise's Hotel during his stay. He passed way in 1973 and is interred at Calvary Cemetery in Los Angeles, California.

NELSON'S NAVAL PURSER

The tales of Admiral Lord Horatio Nelson's heroism and untimely death at the Battle of Trafalgar during the Napoleonic War are well known. On

School children laying flowers at the grave of Walter Burke at the centenary of the Battle of Trafalgar on October 21, 1805. (*Image courtesy of Wouldham Parish Council*)

21 October 1805, when Nelson lay dying after a fatal injury on board HMS *Victory*, he was comforted Limerick man Walter Burke. The *Globe* newspaper quotes Nelson saying to Burke, 'I expect to see every man in his station, and if we succeed today, you and I will go to sea no more.'

The Battle of Trafalgar and the death of Nelson have been commemorated in painting, books and film, and Burke's presence has been noted in many of these. It is believed that Walter Burke was born in 1736 in the county town of Bruff. He followed in an older relative's footsteps and joined the navy as a young man, quickly finding his way to the role of purser. The purser of a navy ship was responsible for handling all the finances on board, and he also oversaw the purchasing of all goods and supplies. Additionally, they were responsible for the general upkeep of a ship, supervising and paying for any repairs that were needed while in port.

Burke joined the *Victory* on 18 April 1804. It is not surprising given his position that he was the oldest member of Nelson's crew. Not long after the Battle of Trafalgar, Burke retired to the sleepy little village of Wouldham, near Rochester in Kent.

Burke would just see the end of the Napoleonic War, having passed away at the age of 79 on 12 September 1815, a few short months after the Battle of Waterloo. His headstone in Wouldham church states that he was 'Purser on his majesty's ship Victory in the glorious battle of Trafalgar and in his arms the immortal Nelson died'. He is also not forgotten in his last home, having a road named in his honour. Traditionally, local school children lay a flower at his grave each year to mark Trafalgar Day.

THE ODD FELLOWS SOCIETY

The Odd Fellows Society was founded in the early nineteenth century. It was an association that took on the role of an insurance policy, where the members would pay a subscription for the society to aid members at times of distress. This was in a time before social welfare, when the care from one of these societies could keep a member out of the workhouse. In 1860, the society was so popular that there were three branches in Limerick; one covering the city, one for the county and the third called Banks of Shannon Old Fellows.

One day in August 1863, the Cork, Waterford and Ennis branches of the Odd Fellows Society arrived in Limerick to spend the day with their Limerick counterparts. When the Cork contingent arrived at the station, the members of the other three counties met them. From here the group marched with standards in hand and wearing their insignia down Queen Street, past Tait's Clock, down Glenworth Street, on to O'Connell Street, and finally ending their procession at McNay's Hotel on William Street. This was undoubtedly an unusual sight for the residents of the city.

It was not all sweetness and light in the Odd Fellows Society. A case came before the Limerick City Petty Sessions after two members came to blows. According to James O'Halloran, his society brother John Peel had interrupted him during a meeting at the society Lodge. O'Halloran called Peel to order, but he responded that he was in order and rushed over to O'Halloran, punching him in the eye. He threw his glove at O'Halloran and proclaimed, 'If you are a man here I challenge you.' After speaking to witnesses, the court imposed a fine of £1 plus court costs on Peel.

OLYMPIC HONOURS

In 1896 Athens, the modern Olympic Games began. At this time, only men could compete in the forty-three events across nine sports and no one from Limerick participated in these first games. It was not until 1924 that Ireland represented itself through Limerick-born athletes who took part under the flags of the United Kingdom and the United States of America.

There were two Limerick-born medal winners at the 1900 Paris games. The hammer throw was the event of choice for John Flanagan, who was born in Kilbreedy but won gold medals for the United States in the 1900 Paris, 1904 St Louis and 1908 London games. Patrick Leahy from Cregan, near Charleville, brought two medals back to Ireland under the flag of the United Kingdom at the 1900 Paris games. He received the silver in high jump and bronze in the long jump. Athleticism was obviously in the Leahy family, as Patrick's older brother, Con, joined him at the 1904 St Louis games, where they competed against each other in the high jump, earning themselves joint silver medals.

Two other local men joined Flanagan on the podium at the 1908 London games. Timothy Ahearne of Athea took part in two events: the triple jump, in which he placed first, and the hurdles, where he missed out on a medal. The 1908 games had a marksman event called 'running deer shooting'. Unsurprisingly, it was a well-to-do member of Limerick society, William Russell Lane-Joynt, a barrister, who brought back the silver. Both Ahearne and Lane-Joynt participated under the flag of the United Kingdom.

The hammer throw was one of Limerick's strongest sports. At the 1920 Antwerp games, Patrick James Ryan, born in Old Pallas, took the gold in the hammer throw and silver in the 56lb weight throw back to his adopted country, the United States. A fellow resident in the US and participant in the 1920 games was Dan Ahearne, younger brother of Timothy Ahearne, who took home gold in 1908.

Ireland carried a flag for the first time at the 1924 Paris games and John O'Grady from Ballybricken was given the honour of carrying it. He went on to represent Ireland in the shot put, where he placed seventeenth. This, along with his other sporting achievements, caused a monument to be erected in his honour on the Ballysimon Road.

A young Limerick doctor, Denis Cussen, sprinted in the 1928 Amsterdam games. Although he won his 100m heat, he placed fifth in the quarter-final. Cussen would return to the Olympics in 1956 Melbourne as a medical officer to the British team.

On 6 June, 1894 race meet for the Limerick Amateur Athletics and Bicycle Club was held at the Market Field. (*Image courtesy of the Limerick Museum*)

As the century drew on, the Limerick participants went from feats of strength to those of endurance. James Hogan, born in Croom, ran the 10,000m and the marathon twice. The first time he ran under the Irish flag in 1964 in Tokyo, then under the flag of the United Kingdom in the 1968 Mexico games. The only Irish man to win the Boston City Marathon, Neil Cusack, competed in the 1972 Munich and 1976 Montreal games. He ran the 10,000m in the first games and the marathon in the second. Niall O'Shaughnessy also ran in 1976 in Montreal in the 800m and 1,500m events.

The 1980s saw four Limerick people participating in the Olympic Games. First, Michael O'Shea ran and placed tenth in the 5,000m in 1980 in Moscow. Frank O'Mara participated in the 1984 Los Angeles games, and placed thirty-third in the 5,000m in 1988 in Seoul. His highest achievement in the Olympics came at the 1992 Barcelona games, where he placed eighteenth in the 5,000m. Barbara Johnson competed in the 400m hurdles in Seoul. Finally, in the 1980s, Gerard Mullins, along with his trusty steeds Rockbarton and Glendalough, participated in equestrian events in the 1984 and 1988 games.

Tom Comyns was part of the Irish relay team in the 2000 Sydney games, while Rosemary Ryan of Bilboa A.C. ran the 5,000m that same year. An adopted Limerick man, Andy Lee, boxed at the 2004 Athens games. Although Lee was born in England, he was raised in Castleconnell. Sean O'Neill rowed for Ireland in 2008 Beijing and his adopted home of New Zealand in 2012

London games. Sam Lynch rowed at both the 1996 Atlanta and 2004 Athens games. Lynch's wife, fellow rower Sinead Jennings, took part in the 2016 Rio de Janeiro games in the lightweight women's double scull. Though she was born in Donegal, she has made Limerick her home and rows with St Michael's Rowing Club in the heart of the city. Finally, Fiona Doyle also participated in Rio in 2016 in the 100m breaststroke.

ODE TO THE OFFICIALS

Today it is commonplace to see smear campaigns against anyone running for the government on social media. However, although the means and medium for spreading false information has changed, the act of doing it has been in practice for centuries. During the third race for President in the United States of America, the challenger Thomas Jefferson accused President Adams of having a 'hideous hermaphroditical character, which has neither the force nor firmness of a man nor the gentleness and sensibility of a woman'.

Limerick was no different when it came to this form of slander, although the means of sharing the misinformation was very different. Ireland is known as the Land of Saints and Scholars, a land of people renowned for their quick wit and lyrical disposition, and in the 1860s there were several ballad singers in the city. The most famous of these was Michael Hogan, the Bard of Thomond, and it was common practice for him to lampoon those in power, especially those who did not pay him.

Two other ballad singers were Thomas Walsh and Terence O'Driscoll of Curry Lane. These two men would wax lyrical to the highest bidder. Their witty words were published and performed throughout the city.

Hiring these men came at a cost, and as shown here, it was wise to pay it. Timothy Morrissey of Clare Street, a clerk in Russell's on Henry Street, hired the two men during the 1865 elections. He wanted them to perform ballads in favour of his candidate, the liberal Francis William Russell, and to belittle his Conservative rival James Spaight.

Walsh and O'Driscoll sang in public for twelve days before the election and printed 600 copies of their song. The bards' fees were 5*s* a day each, and £5 if Russell won the election. When they tried to get their dues, Morrissey refused. In response, the pair took him to court for unpaid fees of £6 6*s*.

At the court, O'Driscoll produced a ditty called Poet's Lament:

This 1888 image of O'Connell Street, then George's Street, shows a bustling city. (*Image courtesy of the National Library of Ireland*)

My name is O'Driscoll
A singer by trade;
Myself and my comrade
We never were paid.

The judge berated the poets and questioned them as to why they thought it was right to get paid for exciting animosity. O'Driscoll replied that he was paid to do just that. It was revealed in the court that two ballad singers could do more to raise excitement and cause violence than any speeches given by the running candidates.

The judge did not agree with the process of slander that was conducted during an election and thought the mobs that resulted from a rowdy ballad did more harm to society than the two men not getting paid. He dismissed the case, stating that the poets were lucky he was not having them arrested.

OBSERVATORY

While the stars above the city today are marred by street lights and pollution, Richard Wallace, a budding astronomer, decided to create his observatory in the heart of the city. Wallace was a silversmith and jeweller by trade. When he opened his new house and store on O'Connell Street in 1841, he added an unusual glass structure on to the roof. The observatory was not the only addition to his building; he also incorporated a large clock into its façade. The face of the clock read *Tempus Fugit* (Time Flies).

It is not surprising that Wallace sought solitude in the stars as he and his wife Bridget Bunton had a total of thirteen children. Wallace outlived only three of his children, so it would undoubtedly have been a very busy household.

Wallace sent his temperature, air pressure readings and observations into the local press daily. On hearing about a hot-air balloon flight across the city in 1849, he gave the pilot, Hampden W. Russell, a barometer to assist him in gaining the highest altitude.

Wallace passed away on 21 May 1875 at his residence, 88 O'Connell Street. He left his wife, Bridget, effects of just under £30,000, a large fortune even by today's standard. It was enough for his wife to live on comfortably for almost twenty years. His business passed to his son, John Henry Wallace.

Wallace's observatory above his store on O'Connell Street. (*Author's collection*)

PHENOMENAL PIANO PLAYING

Swizz-born Sigismond Thalberg was one of the most famous pianists of the nineteenth century, although today he is far lesser known than his Hungarian counterpart, Franz Liszt. Thalberg paid four visits to Limerick, while Liszt only came once. Liszt performed in Limerick during the second week of January 1841. While in Limerick, he stayed in the home of Major Vokes in Pery Square. The *Limerick Chronicle* of 13 January 1841 wrote of his performance, 'M. Liszt's concert on Monday evening brought a full and fashionable audience. As a performer on the Piano, he is powerful, rapid, and brilliant.' Such was the 'impress of his execution that several thought the instrument would fall to pieces in his hands'.

Thalberg's first visit to Limerick came in 1837 when he was 25 years old. Before his performance, a letter was published singing his praise:

> It is enough that I tell you no instrument of the general kind is sufficient to exhibit the extraordinary powers of this wonderful man. I have therefore forwarded, per *Ariel*, a Grand Piano Fort for his use. Thalberg must be heard, for I assure you words cannot convey the very faintest idea of his performance. Yours, W.F. Collard.

The concert took place on 30 December 1837. Joining the pianist were singers Mr J. Bennett and Mr Berettoni. It was not noted in the press where in Limerick this concert took place, but the ticket agent for all Thalberg's Limerick concerts was Messrs Corbett & Sons. In 1837, Corbett was based at 38 Patrick Street and the tickets cost 7*s*. The Corbett brothers, James and Patrick, ran a music store in Limerick from at least 1824.

There was some confusion on the night of the concert as the three unison patent grand pianos shipped to Limerick for the performance arrived three days too late. Despite this, the show was a resounding success and Thalberg received £75.

Two years later he returned to Limerick, on 4 October 1839, to give a 'grand farewell morning concert'. Also performing with him was Dublin-born opera singer and composer Michael William Balfe and his wife, Hungarian-born soprano Lina Roser.

There was then a gap of over twenty years as Thalberg travelled the world performing. He arrived back in Limerick to play the Athenaeum on Cecil Street on 20 November 1862. Among the numbers he played that night were *Tarantella, Home Sweet Home* and *Fantasia.* He returned the following year and gave his last pianoforte recital in the Athenaeum. Not only was this the last time that Thalberg appeared in Limerick but the last year that he performed in public. He passed away eight years later in Naples, Italy.

A PECULIAR PERFORMANCE

Thalberg was not the only pianist to play in Limerick. Although the pianist that performed on 1 November 1953 gave a rather peculiar show. That day Marie Aston, or 'Musical Marie', attempted to break the world record for time playing the piano. Marie played for 134 hours non-stop in the Catholic Institute on Sarsfield Street. A ticket to see her cost an adult £1 and children 6*d*. Opening hours for the public were between 9 a.m. and midnight, while police and press were always permitted to attend.

Aston ended the night with the National Anthem. Members of the St John's Ambulance had to help her move from her stool to a couch. She was then taken by ambulance to Cruise's Hotel. There were over 3,000 people on the street as she finished playing. This crowd caused damage to cars, including caving in the roofs as some men climbed on them to get a better view of the pianist. Limerick Steamship Company and Philip J. Murray of Cork attempted to claim damages from the Limerick Corporation for the wreckage caused to their vehicles.

PIMPS AND HOUSES OF ILL REPUTE

Brothels were not uncommon in nineteenth-century Limerick. According to the *Limerick Reporter* on 11 March 1845, there were sixteen brothels in Post

Office Lane alone. These brothels, or 'houses of ill repute', were unhampered by the police unless they caused a public disturbance.

One such problem occurred in October 1859 at a brothel in Westland Street near the docks. The disturbance led to the arrest of Margaret Sheehy, charged with the assault of Margaret Maher. The stout middle-aged Sheehy was the owner of the brothel. The jury dismissed the case for assault but found Sheehy guilty of keeping a brothel. As this was her second time in court for the same charge, the judge sentenced her to two years in prison and a fine of 20*s*.

In 1844, 36-year-old Francis Forrest found himself on the wrong side of the law. His crime was 'sleeping in a brothel' and his punishment was twelve months in jail with hard labour.

Another case before the courts in July 1893 was rather strange. This case surrounded a 30-year-old educated woman, Elizabeth Christianson of Thomas Street. Her husband was employed in Cleeve's Condensed Milk Factory, but he had separated from her as she had been acting 'immorally'. Despite this, he hired a solicitor, James H. Moran, to represent his wife.

The arrest came about after a Father Creagh became aware that Christianson was inviting married women back to her house and offering their services to men in exchange for money. In a shocking turn of events, on the second day of the trial, Moran quit his role as defence for the accused. He explained to the court that after hearing the testimony from the witnesses the previous day he was in no doubt over the guilt of his client.

The jury also agreed with Moran. In their closing statement they scolded the Welsh-born Christianson as her act was not out of need for financial security but out of pure mischief. After her background was considered, she was sentenced to three months' hard labour.

PAYING THE ROUNDS

During Holy Week in 1881, Mary Kearney of Colooney Street, now Wolfe Tone Street, undertook a very unusual form of employment. The work came about when the health of Edmond Fitzgerald of Hartstonge Street was failing due to an unspecified illness. After trying all the traditional methods open to him at the time and watching each fail, he spoke to his servant and a Mrs Kennedy of Hartstonge Street to see what options they had.

The women suggested Mary Kearney to 'pay rounds' (say prayers) at St Patrick's Well. After receiving a large cross from Fitzgerald's house, Mary

Well-dressed visitors to St Patrick's Well, Singland, *c.* 1900. (*Image courtesy of the Limerick Museum*)

began her pilgrimage. Despite the miserable weather, she prayed at and collected water from the holy well in old brandy bottles. The holy water was taken to the ailing man and was poured over his head and shoulders.

It was even odder that Fitzgerald asked for this ritual to be performed since he was a Protestant and according to his faith holy water had no power. Despite the prayers and water, Fitzgerald's health remained the same, so he refused to pay her for services rendered. He offered her 3*s*, but this was laughed at as it was not enough to buy fuel to dry her clothes.

Later that year, Kearney took the old man to the Limerick City Petty Sessions, where the judges unanimously awarded 15*s* and costs. This award was given not because of the healing powers of the waters in St Patrick's Well, but because Kearney carried out the task for which she was employed. Fitzgerald never did get his cure but would live for another two years to the fine age of 94.

THE QUEEN'S POETESS

In 1839, a young Limerick woman, Isabella Jackson, publicly criticised Queen Victoria. Jackson was a 19-year-old poet living in the city with her parents, Joseph and Mary Jackson. In the late summer of 1839, some of her poems were published.

The most notable of these was 'Lines on the death of Lady Flora Hastings'. This poem delved into the life and death of Lady Flora Hastings, a lady-in-waiting at the royal household, who was accused of adultery when her stomach began to swell. She was forced to undergo a virginity test, which she passed. Tragically the young woman was suffering from a growth on her liver, which proved fatal. The Hastings family were distraught and demanded an apology from the new Queen, but this apology never came.

Back in Limerick, Jackson was struck by this tragedy. Her poem struck a chord with wealthy ladies in London, who sent an elegant gold watch and a suit of jewellery to the poetess. These gifts were sent care of the *Limerick Chronicle*, as the ladies in London had no other means to contact Jackson.

Despite her lash out at the crown, Jackson would pen a verse on the nuptials of Queen Victoria and Prince Albert in 1840. Two of her poems were published in the local press in February of that year, the first called 'The Tears of Memory' and the second a lament at the death of Limerick Alderman D.F.G. Mahony. The funeral cortege of the alderman was quite extravagant, with eight female members of his household staff draped in long white cloaks leading the procession. Following these women were the representatives of the local trades in white scarves and hatbands. Only then did the hearse make an appearance, followed by members of the clergy, the mayor, the sheriffs and their many attendants. Forty-eight private carriages were bringing up the rear.

In the spring of 1841, Jackson would step on to the stage at Swinburn's Great Rooms, Sarsfield Street. The advertisements leading up to her show mentioned that she was patronised by 'Her Most Gracious Majesty', so all ills caused by her poem two years prior had been forgiven. During the performance, she presented her new poem about the newly born Princess Victoria. She repeated the lecture in McDowell's Rooms at the Imperial Hotel, Cork, later that year.

Jackson never married. She worked as a teacher until she was about 50 years old, when she developed an unnamed brain disease. This debilitation caused her to be committed in the then Limerick Lunatic Asylum, Mulgrave Street where, in 1890, she passed away.

QUEENSTOWN QUARTERS

Charlotte Grace O'Brien was born on 23 November 1845, into a staunch nationalist family in Cahermoyle, between Newcastle West and Foynes. When she was only 3 years old her father, William Smith O'Brien, was convicted of sedition for his part in the Young Irelander Rebellion of 1848, a failed Irish nationalist uprising. For his role O'Brien was sentenced to the Tasmanian penal colony. He eventually returned to Limerick in 1856. This disturbed upbringing would most certainly have left an impression on young Charlotte.

Following her father's death in 1864, Charlotte moved in with her widowed brother to assist in the raising of his children until he remarried in 1880. She then moved to Foynes. Her hearing became progressively worse as she aged, and she became entirely deaf while still a young woman. Despite this, she continued in her father's footsteps, fighting for equality.

Charlotte's fight was for the poor emigrants of Ireland, especially those who were female. She witnessed the slums developing around Queenstown, now Cobh, in Cork, and was made aware of the dangerous position this put the young migrant women in when seeking accommodation while waiting to board ships bound for America and Australia.

On the back of this, in 1882, she founded a boarding house that could sleep 105. Sadly, the boarding house failed as local merchants, who were affiliated with other boarding houses, boycotted it.

O'Brien often made the arduous journey to America to report on the conditions of the poor travellers. Her interest also lay in the conditions these young women were arriving into in New York and arranged for a priest to aid them. Through her contact with the clergy in New York, a boarding house

A view of Foynes harbour in 1955. This was used as a landing strip for flying boats from 1937 until 1946. (*Image courtesy of the* Limerick Leader)

was established to assist the Irish immigrants to adjust to their new lives in the United States.

O'Brien would continue her work on both sides of the Atlantic until ill-health forced her to retire. In 1887, she renounced her faith and joined the Roman Catholic Church. She continued to live in Foynes until her death in 1909.

QUEEN OF CORSICA

Following the Siege of Limerick in 1691, the Jacobites were given the option to go into exile. Those who took up this offer were known as the Wild Geese. Two of those who left were Dominick and David Sarsfield, the sons of the 3rd Viscount of Kilmallock. Their home in the town was where the Friars Gate Theatre stands today on Sarsfield Street.

Dominick, the eldest, inherited the family title and lands. In 1689, to keep the wealth in the family, he married his distant cousin, Anne Sarsfield of Lucan.

Anne was the sister of the famous Patrick Sarsfield, who led the Jacobite Army in Limerick. After the Jacobite defeat in Limerick and the signing of the Treaty of Limerick, the Sarsfields lost their lands and titles and relocated to France.

The brothers settled into their new lives on the Continent. Three years later, Catalina Sarsfield, the eldest of David's six daughters, was born in Nantes, France. The brothers continued to serve in the military to a fatal end. Dominick was killed in 1701 at the Battle of Chiari. Nine years later, after relocating to Spain, David was killed at the Battle of Villaviciosa.

At this time Catalina was a young teen. Although she was left fatherless, David Sarsfield had forged important links with the European royalty. Queen Elisabetta of Spain, who was only a few years older than Catalina, invited the girl into the court to act as a maid of honour.

Unsurprisingly, the royal court played host to a wide range of individuals from around the world. One adventurer, Theodore von Neuhoff German, arrived in the court and in 1718, Catalina fell for him. Shortly after, the Queen granted permission for the young couple to be married.

Alas, the marriage was not a happy one. Theodore found his new wife to be stubborn and bad-tempered, while Catalina was disappointed at her new husband's lack of income, her being a woman accustomed to expensive tastes. It took only a year for the marriage to fracture and was concluded when Theodore took a selection of Catalina's jewels and absconded to Paris without her. Four years later, Catalina went to find her husband in Paris. Here she continued her role as a maid of honour in the French court.

Catalina was amazed to discover that her husband had racked up debts with his elaborate spending on clothing and parties. He convinced Catalina to sell her pension from Queen Elisabetta to pay his debtors, after which he left her and his then young daughter in Paris to continue to roam Europe on his own.

During a stay in Genoa, Theodore met with some Corsican rebels. Through the art of persuasion that he had mastered in his years as an adventurer, Theodore convinced them to proclaim him King of Corsica to free the country. He arrived in Corsica in March 1736 and was quickly crowned King Theodore I. He followed through on his promise to the rebels and began talks with the Spanish royal family to grant him rule over the new state. Despite his previous interactions with Spain, permission was granted, and his title became official.

As the wife of the King of Corsica, Catalina, the daughter of a Limerick man, became the Queen, although she never set foot in the country. King Theodore I soon bored of the role and after only seven months as monarch he absconded on his hunt for fame and fortune once more. Eventually, his mounting debts caught up with him and he was imprisoned in London. He died on 11 December 1756, soon after his release. He was buried in St Anne's Church in London, where his memorial reads, 'Near this place is interred Theodore King of Corsica who died in this parish ....'

As for the former Queen of Corsica, Catalina, she remained in Paris, where one of the final mentions of her was in the dedication of a novel in 1736. It is believed that she passed away in 1759. Catalina must have remained in contact with Queen Elisabetta as her daughter, the Princess of Corsica, later returned to the Spanish court.

RUMMAGING FOR A ROYAL WIFE

There were several royal visits to Limerick over the centuries, but the visit of 1828 was very unusual. The royal in question was born Count Hermann Pückler on 30 October 1785, and later gained the extravagant name of Prince Hermann Ludwig Heinrich von Pückler-Muskau. His first marriage took place in 1817 to Lucie von Pappenheim, but this was not successful and in 1826 the marriage was dissolved.

As his former wife was the wealthiest of the pair, it left the Prince in a predicament. He needed to locate a new wealthy spouse to fund his expensive taste. To this end, he began a grand tour of the United Kingdom and Ireland. His Irish tour began in Dublin in August 1828, moving quickly to Galway. He was not impressed by the Galwegians, comparing them to savages.

The Prince then arrived in Limerick. One of the Catholic churches rang their bells to mark his entry to the city. The caretaker of the church would later locate the Prince at the Moriarty Hotel, 7 O'Connell Street, and ask for 10*s* for that honour. Later that day a member of the Protestant church warned the Prince against giving donations to the Catholic Church but in the same breath, he asked for a donation to the Protestant poor house.

The aesthetic of the city appealed to the Prince. He would later write that the 'Gothic churches and moss-covered ruins; with dark narrow streets, and curious houses of various dates' appealed to his romantic nature. He also applauded the busy markets and surrounding countryside.

As with all visitors to Limerick, he went to see the Treaty Stone. Here he was greeted by some locals cheering 'Long life to Napoleon!' These locals believed that Hermann was the son of Napoleon Bonaparte. He scoffed at the idea and called back, 'You joke! I am at least ten years too old to be the son of the great emperor and the beautiful princess.'

Two clubs, the Limerick Independent Club and the Order of Liberators, invited the Prince to dinner, where they were to induct him as an honorary member. The royal missed this meal as he was on his way to Kerry to stay with Daniel O'Connell, the Liberator.

The Prince's search for a new wife was unsuccessful but his exuberant personality is remembered in Europe through his gardens, writings and ice cream in Germany.

RATHKEALE AND SIR WALTER RALEIGH

In the fifteenth century, Castle Matrix was built on the outskirts of Rathkeale town by the Fitzgerald family. The castle passed through many hands before resting with the Southwell family after Sir Nicholas Malby burned the town of Rathkeale to the ground in 1579.

In 1580, the Elizabethan poet Edmond Spenser and adventurer Sir Walter Raleigh visited the Southwells at Castle Matrix. Raleigh received the freedom of the town that year after the defeat of John, Earl of Desmond.

After this meeting, Spenser wrote 'The Faerie Queen', one of the longest poems in the English language. He mentions Raleigh in the dedications. This was one of Raleigh's many visits to Rathkeale as he was close friends with Edmund Southwell. During one of his later stays, he presented Southwell with a gift from the Americas, Virginia Tubers. These were planted around the castle and in 1610, the crop of Irish-grown potatoes was harvested. The resulting potatoes were distributed throughout the land.

An ivy-covered Castle Matrix Rathkeale from 1912. (*Image courtesy of the Limerick Museum*)

A century later, one of Edmund Southwell's descendants, Thomas Southwell, rescued dozens of Palantine families from Germany. These families were settled in the grounds of the castle and their descendants remain in the area to this day.

ROMANCE IN A RURAL VILLAGE

Henry Fox-Strangway, the heir of the 1st Earl of Ilchester, was posted to Limerick as a young soldier. As a dashing young man in his twenties, the future Earl was invited to many high-society events. It was at one of these events, a hunt ball, he met Mary Theresa O'Grady.

The young debutant was the daughter of Standish O'Grady of Cappercullen, near Murroe. As young love blossomed and the two courted, Standish began to worry. Although his family were not poor, they were also not members of the aristocracy. Fearing a scandal, he wrote to Fox-Strangway's father, insisting that his son be removed from Limerick at once.

Sadly, his plan worked, and the lovers were torn apart. Soon after this Standish received a letter from the Earl commending him for his actions regarding their children. He also informed him that an acquaintance, Colonel Prendergast, would be passing through Limerick and sought permission to stop at Murroe.

The colonel arrived and stayed a week. The elderly gent looked kindly on young Mary, who he saw as thoughtful, and she would take walks with him. As the week came to an end, the colonel took Standish aside and asked if Mary would be better suited to a warmer climate, as she seemed pale and sullen at times.

Standish informed the colonel of his daughter's broken heart and that only time was the cure. The colonel insisted that he inform the Earl at once as he was sure he would approve the match. Standish hesitated to say he was sure the Earl would never allow his son to marry a poor Irish girl. The colonel laughed long and hard, much to Standish's confusion. Finally, the colonel confessed. He was the Earl in disguise and would be delighted to have his son marry such a charming young woman.

The date was set, and the pair married in Abington Church in 1772. They lived together for twenty years, raising four children, before Mary's untimely death in 1792.

RISING RELIGION

Three of the Palantine families that arrived at the Southwell estate in 1709 were that of Ruckle, Embury and Heck. In 1734, Barbara Ruckle was born into this community. After her marriage to Paul Heck, she became Barbara Heck. She had a close friendship with cousin Philip Embury, a carpenter, who was five years her senior. He was born in Ballingrane and married Margaret Switzer of Rathkeale.

John Wesley, the founder of the Methodist movement, arrived in Limerick in 1752 to spread the word about his new religion. Both Heck and Embury attended the meeting and quickly converted. Embury took on the role of lay minister for the fledgling Methodist community in Ballingrane and Barbara Heck was one of the most enthusiastic members of the congregation.

In 1760, the emigrant ship *Pery* left Limerick city from the quays at the Custom House. Passengers included the Heck and Embury families destined for the New World. After an arduous journey across the ocean, they arrived in New York, which was then a small city of only 18,000 inhabitants.

For a period after their arrival, dazzled by the newness of their situation, their religious observance decreased. One night, Heck discovered her fellow emigrants, including Embury, gambling. She tossed the cards into the fire and scolded them. She called on Embury to preach but he would not as he had no

The 1734 birth place Barbara Heck, Ballingrane. (*Image courtesy of* Limerick Leader)

church and no congregation. She insisted that if he began to preach she would find his congregation.

There were only five people in attendance at the first meeting of the Wesleyan Society on 12 October 1766, in a loft space. Within two years they had outgrown this space and erected a church on John Street, in what is now the heart of the financial district surrounded by skyscrapers. The church still holds the original lectern built by Embury for use in the loft.

In 1818, their small wooden blue chapel was replaced by one of stone. The church that stands today was erected in 1841 and was designated a New York City Landmark in 1964, being added to the National Register of Historic Places in 1973. It is known as the Mother Church of American Methodism.

Embury continued to preach each Sunday but hung up his carpentry tools for those of a flax grower in Camden Valley, New York. In 1775, he was wounded in a mowing accident and tragically succumbed to his injuries.

Heck travelled with her husband and five children throughout the north-west of the country, spreading her mission. She moved across the border to Canada and founded the first congregation there. In 1804, she passed away peacefully with her Bible in her lap.

Her memory is marked in her John Street Church each week with the lighting of a pair of her candlesticks. Their homes in Ballingrane are noted historical locations and the anniversaries of the founding of their church is marked locally. Also, in 1766, a Methodist church was erected in Ballingrane that now bears the name of the Embury Heck Church.

S

SURPRISING STATUES

An 1908 image of Sarsfield Statue in the grounds of St John's Cathedral. (*Image courtesy of the Limerick Museum*)

Statues usually stand stately in their environment with the muses gazing out over the world, but Limerick took a decidedly different approach to the erection of statues. The earliest statue portraying a living person in Limerick City is that of Sir Thomas Spring Rice.

Spring Rice sits atop a pillar in the centre of the People's Park. Unusually for a monument of this kind, Spring Rice was still alive and only 38 years old at the time of its production. Henry Aaron Baker designed the sculpture and Thomas Kirk designed the pillar. Kirk is known for his sculpture of Admiral Horatio Nelson that once stood on top of Nelson's Pillar in Dublin.

A rival to Spring Rice in his political career was Daniel O'Connell, The Liberator. His statue on O'Connell Avenue is situated the same way O'Connell did in life, facing away from Spring Rice. On 15 August 1857, the monument by sculptor John Hogan was unveiled. It was the first outdoor statue erected to The Liberator.

A monument to Patrick Sarsfield had been in discussion from at least 1845. It would take another thirty-six years before the statue would be constructed and displayed. Why did it take so long? The main point of contention came down to the location of this statue. This is a debate that continues to this day.

The statue, which now stands in the grounds of St John's Cathedral, was outlined by Limerick artist Henry O'Shea and designed by Dublin man John Young. The casting of the bronze memorial was carried out by Young's London Art Foundry.

Although Sarsfield's statue was completed in 1881, debate continued in the Corporation as to a suitable location. In stepped Ambrose Hall, who was one of the initiators of the project. He had his sight set on Pery Square but was outvoted twelve to five. Other members of the Corporation wanted the statue erected in Bank Place.

Meanwhile, the statue sat in storage as the discussion continued for months. Hall, who was disillusioned by the delay, contacted the Bishop of Limerick. After a series of private discussions, Hall convinced the Bishop to allow the statue to be erected in the grounds of St John's Cathedral. Without pomp or ceremony, the statue was placed where it sits today.

SWEETS, SILVER TEETH AND A SIMIAN

Catherine McNamara supplied confectionary to the citizens of Limerick in the 1820s. Her sweetness was not just on the shelves though, as in 1823 she married the much younger John Goggin. Soon Catherine was expecting their first child and Goggin took over the day-to-day activity in the store. Over the next forty years, Goggin would dip into the supply of liqueurs, lozenges, foreign and exotic fruits, leaving a lot to be desired with his oral hygiene.

Goggin had a full set of silver dentures created to replace his own teeth. In 1863, Mary Shaughnessy managed to steal the dentures, passing them off to 12-year-old Margaret Grady. As it was Shaughnessy's twenty-fifth conviction she was sentenced to three months' imprisonment at hard labour. The young girl's sentence was much tougher; after serving two weeks in prison she was sent to St Joseph's Reformatory School in Dublin for five years.

That winter, Goggin's name hit the news again in a bizarre circumstance. A friend had gifted Goggin a monkey, which became a household favourite to all but the family dog. One day, a fight broke out between the dog and the monkey, which resulted in Goggin receiving a bite on the hand while trying to separate the pair.

Although an ointment of sodium hydroxide was placed on the wound, an infection set in and doctors were called a few days later. This was sadly too late for Goggin, who contracted hydrophobia (rabies) and died soon after. As it could not be determined if the illness came from the dog or the monkey, they were both put down. It would take another forty years before rabies was eradicated in Ireland.

SHIPWRECKED IN THE SOUTH SEAS

On a stormy night in 1887, the ship *Derry Castle* crashed on its return journey from Australia to Limerick. The *Derry Castle* had only been built four years earlier for the Limerick company Spaights and Sons. The ship was on a return journey from Australia to Limerick with a cargo full of wheat and a single passenger, Ballyclough-born James McGhie.

Also on board during this fateful night of 20 March 1887, were twenty-three members of the crew. The ship smashed against the rocks on the deserted Enderby Island at two o'clock in the morning and quickly began to sink.

Although the shore was within sight, only seven of the crew and McGhie made it to land. In the following days, the survivors laid those who washed ashore to rest in a makeshift grave marked by the figurehead of the *Derry Castle*. The men began to explore the small rocky island and to their delight found a small hut.

This hut had been erected and stocked with emergency supplies by the New Zealand government to aid those who became shipwrecked. Sadly, everything but a bottle of salt water had been taken before the *Derry Castle*'s accident.

With the hut as a base, the men constructed shelters and waited. They survived on shellfish and the random supplies that washed ashore from the *Derry Castle*. They were able to start a fire by using a piece of cotton in place

The hut and shelters used by the castaways on Enderby Island. The hut reads 'For castaways only'. Photographed by William Dougall soon after the castaways returned to Australia in 1887. (*Image courtesy of the National Museum of New Zealand*)

of a bullet in a cartridge that McGhie found in his pocket. They struck the cartridge with a stone, which caused a spark to ignite the cotton. The men were overjoyed at the ability to cook their catch.

The months passed and all hope of rescue seemed lost, but on day ninety-two an axe head was found. This was used to build a crude boat the survivors named the *Derry Castle Punt*. It was large enough for two of the men to travel to a nearby government outpost at Erebus Cove, on the coast of Auckland Island. Luckily, this hut had not been looted and the other six men later joined them.

On 19 July 1887, all eight men were rescued at Erebus Cove by a poacher's ship on its way to hunt seals. This was not the end of their adventure though, as the ship back to Australia was almost lost. They landed back in Australia on 21 September 1887, ending an incredible adventure for a Limerick man.

McGhie had enough excitement in the Southern Hemisphere and returned to Limerick, where he worked as an auctioneer until his death in 1903. He was buried in his family grave at St Munchin's Church of Ireland graveyard. The *Derry Castle* figurehead was removed from Enderby Island to the Canterbury Museum, Christchurch, New Zealand. The site where the men were stranded for all those months was renamed the Derry Castle Cove and a permanent memorial was erected to the men who lost their lives.

A SPIRIT WITH THE SPIRITS

Walking around the walls of St John's Graveyard in Limerick city, there is a break in the masonry where a building stands. The building at the corner of John Street and the aptly named Church Street has been used in most recent years as an off licence. It is remarkable that alcohol is sold virtually in the grounds of a church.

How did this strange mixing of the spirits and the spirit begin? The story goes back to the eighteenth century when in the 1740s a house was erected by the church sexton. The sexton, John Murray, did not get along with the curate of St John's Church. The curate decided that Murray's services were no longer required and sent him notice to quit the house along with his job.

Murray did not appreciate being told to leave the house he built. Interestingly, his grandfather, also called John Murray, built the arch that stood behind the building in the church wall in 1693. So, Murray felt a strong connection to the site and he decided to take the curate to court. The magistrates judged that the firing of Murray was fair but the removal of him from his house was not.

Despite his former employer, Murray opened a public house in the building. The public house boomed and would continue in that vein for over 260 years. The original building was knocked down and replaced in the 1980s but the tradition of selling spirits with the spirits continued.

T

TEA-TOTALLING TEMPERANCE

The temperance movement began in Ireland in the 1840s with Father Theobald Mathew leading the charge. Mathew was born just over the Tipperary border in Golden in 1790. He would visit Limerick city often, as his brother-in-law William Dunbar ran a provision store in Michael Street. Mathew was no stranger to the county towns and villages, paying particular attention to the east of the county. Although Mathew was ordained at 24 years old, it would take until 1838 before he found his niche with the Cork Total Abstinence Society. The word of this society quickly spread, and it had amassed over 150,000 members within a year.

The first temperance society in Limerick was in St Michael's parish in 1839. This was quickly followed by St John's parish Temperance Society, based on Charlotte's Quay. While attending the races in 1839, the Mayor of Limerick noted that not one of the members of the temperance movement had broken their pledge. The rise may have come from some highly publicised cases of death and disfigurement attributed to alcohol. In 1839, Michael Greatrakes became so intoxicated that he fell into the fire of his home at Hogg's Lane in the city, where he suffered terrible burns to his torso. Later that year on Military Road (O'Connell Avenue), a man called Murphy was found dead from alcohol poisoning. In Knockainy the following year, Maurice Fitzgerald drove his horse and cart while drunk, breaking his back, when he crashed.

In 1840, a Scottish periodical, *Tait's Edinburgh Magazine*, interviewed several Limerick members of the movement to find out the reasons why they took the pledge. A 54-year-old tanner named John Leonard claimed that he and his wife used to drink whiskey. He went on to tell the magazine that before he took the pledge he did not have a pot to boil a dozen potatoes, but when he and his wife moved to Cork where they took the pledge, they finally lived quite comfortably.

Michael Downes, a 60-year-old horse breaker and jockey, went to Fr Mathew in November 1839 as 'he couldn't keep himself from drinking'. As a jockey, he could earn as much as twenty guineas in three days, but he would drink it all and for the following four days would not have money for food. He developed pains and aches and always felt uneasy until he could get to the whiskey. After abstaining for five months he stated that he 'had no more idea of taking whiskey than vitriol [sulphuric acid]'.

Sixty-seven-year-old cooper John Hogan claimed that he drank hard for many years. He had no shoes and could not even afford straw for his children to use as a bed. He had previously joined a Temperance Society and stayed away from alcohol for eight years until the cholera epidemic of 1833. He had been recommended wine negus (a type of mulled wine), which he thought so nasty that he put whiskey into it to drink it. For the next four years he drank as hard as before, but then took a personal vow against alcohol.

Two navy pensioners, 68-year-old Stephen Lyddy and 46-year-old John Normile, also gave up the demon drink. Lyddy confessed that he would drink

A relaxed day on Mathew Bridge at the turn of the nineteenth century. (*Image courtesy of the National Library of Ireland*)

three half-pints of whiskey instead of drinking milk, while Normile did not own a coat and barely had 'a shirt to his back'. James Coleman would have whiskey for breakfast, causing the 48-year-old to age prematurely.

Every Monday morning William O'Brien, a sawyer, would pawn his coat to pay for his weekly alcohol. After taking the pledge he said he felt 25 instead of 51. Sixty-four-year-old Patrick MacNamara and his brothers all took the pledge in 1839. The brothers were all fishermen and Patrick spoke for them, claiming they could now bear the wet and cold of their occupation better without spirits.

On Sunday, 3 July 1842, Fr Mathew arrived in the parish of Abington and Murroe on the invitation of the local parish priest, Rev. Dr Thomas O'Brien Costello. He was there to host a meeting of the Temperance Society. The meeting took place in Mr Duhig's field at the crossroads in Murroe. In the days leading up to it, Duhig had removed his freshly sown crops from the field. Local builders went out to erect stands, including an altar and a gallery. The local band in Murroe performed from the gallery, while bands from the surrounding towns of Newport, Killaloe, Bruff, Caherconlish and six bands from Limerick city supported them.

A crowd of over 20,000 waited in the field for the arrival of Fr Mathew. During the proceedings of the day, thousands of those in the audience took the pledge against consuming alcohol. Mathew warned those gathered against joining the secret societies, which he claimed were filled with vice, over the Tipperary border in Newport.

After the proceedings concluded and the crowd was dispersed, Fr Matthew returned to Castle Comfort, the home of Rev. Costello, for the night. He donated a large sum of money to the Murroe band before his departure the following morning.

The importance of temperance was passed down through the generations in the Murroe area. In the late 1870s, villagers would occasionally write into a temperance magazine. In 1879, a series of letters appeared in the magazine reprimanding the locals, claiming that a number of individuals in the community, including a parish priest, brought about their deaths by alcohol. It was believed these letters were written by Patrick Dillon.

One summer day that year as Dillon and Archibald J. Nicholl were walking past a field in the village they were spotted by Richard and Michael Laffan. The Laffans ran towards Dillon with their pitchforks in hand calling him a spy. Feeling aggrieved, Dillon brought his accusers to court at the next Murroe Petty Sessions. Unusually, the magistrates dismissed the case against the Laffans as the community had been slighted by Dillion and their anger was deemed justified.

The temperance movement was credited with reducing crime at a dramatic rate across the country. On the death of Fr Mathew, it was stated that the number of murders fell from 247 in 1838 to 105 in 1841. Furthermore, there were twenty faction fights in 1839 but only eight in 1841. Also, jailbreak attempts fell dramatically from thirty-four in 1837 to zero in 1841 and those who were imprisoned fell 12,049 in 1839 to 9,875 by 1845.

TRIALS AND TRIBULATIONS OF TRAVEL

In 1750 there were only four carriages in the city. These belonged to the Bishop, the Dean, a clergyman and a gentleman. By 1770, there were seventy coaches and port chaises. Ten years later there were 183 four-wheeled carriages and 115 two-wheeled carriages in the city and a one-mile radius. The wealthier in the city were also moved by sedan.

Those without a private carriage would have to find other means of travelling between cities. This is where Andrew Buchanan of Thomondgate comes in. He ran stagecoaches from Limerick to Dublin from the mid-eighteenth century. At the time the route between these two cities was perilous, with the roads rough and filled with bandits. Before 1760, passengers intending to travel to Dublin would meet at a coffee house on Quay Lane. Here they would sign up for the journey, which would take five days as the same horses would be used throughout the entire trip.

Buchanan saw flaws in this system and in 1760 he ran his first regular service on 'The Fly' stagecoach after setting up his base on what is now Gerald Griffin Street. The route would travel over Thomond Bridge, to Killaloe, rounding Keeper Hill. He managed to reduce the travel time by a day taking this route. Ten years later he introduced 'The Balloon' stagecoach and changed horses along the route, bringing it down to a three-day journey. Buchanan ran 'The Fly' and 'The Balloon' in a similar fashion for the next twenty years.

Buchanan was not alone in offering this service and 1784 saw a spike in competition. However, Buchanan was not worried about the smaller companies like John Halloran of Thomondgate, who ran a post chaise, a small fast carriage that carried between two and four persons.

It was only when Messrs Foster and Osborne of Dublin began exploiting the route that Buchanan began to worry. Although their journey would take five days, their prices were less than Buchanan's. The local man did not take this threat to his livelihood sitting down and, perhaps through his instigation, the local stagecoach drivers issued a warning to Foster and Osborne not to expand to Limerick. To calm the locals, Foster and Osborne went into partnership with Benjamin Meredith, who moved to Limerick to meet the coaches.

Notices started to appear in the press about highway robbery on Buchanan's carriages, which caused its passengers to become nervous, although these notices were disputed by Buchanan. Tensions began to flair within Foster and Osborne as their man on the ground, Meredith, quit his post on 25 October 1784. Seventeen days later, Meredith sold the company's carriage for half the original cost.

In 1790, Buchanan changed the route through the newly constructed Clare Street towards Nenagh. This change caused the journey to now only take two days and it could be achieved in less than twenty-four hours if necessary. This was an amazing achievement given that the route travelled through bogs and hills in areas where bad weather caused them to become impassable.

As other competitors came and went, Buchanan and his stagecoaches remained. His son Henry would take over the metaphorical reins and lead the company into the nineteenth century.

TRAFFIC LIGHTS

There were cars on the streets of Limerick from the turn of the twentieth century, with the first officially registered in Limerick on New Year's Day 1904. It was a white Renault owned by James Perry Goodbody, the owner of Bannatynes Flour Mill (later Ranks) on the Dock Road.

On 25 May 1908, sixty-three automobiles took part in the hill climb Irish Automobile Club Reliability Trials for Touring Cars in the city. While the 1930s saw three Grand Prix races roar through the city streets. The first of these, in 1935, was known as 'Round the Houses' and had a 2.76-mile route up William Street through Carey's Road around to Rosbrien Road through Punches Cross, and back down O'Connell Street. First place went to Luis Fontes driving an Alfa Romeo.

The 1936 race brought tragedy with the death of John Fitzroy, the 9th Duke of Grafton, while driving a Bugatti. The winner was Alan Hutchinson in an MG. The last Grand Prix of this era took place in 1938 and J. McClure took home the top prize while driving an MG.

Despite this it would take another forty-five years before the first set of traffic lights were turned on in the city. In September 1948 discussions began in the Corporation between Mayor M.B. O'Malley and the city manager over the importance of traffic lights. While the mayor was in favour of the lights and the Corporation's control of them, the city manager believed it was a matter for the Gardai.

One of the members of the council, Councillor Dillon, voiced his concern at the proposed location of the lights at the O'Connell Street–William Street junction. He believed this would cause confusion when funerals were passing through the streets. He stated it would never do to have 'one half of the cortège at the cemetery while the other half would be held up by the traffic lights'. His remarks were greeted with laugher and duly dismissed.

The traffic lights were eventually approved and on 18 July 1949, they were switched on. It took only two days before the first accident happened at the junction. A lorry and Ford car were both attempting to enter Patrick Street, the Ford from William Street and the lorry from Sarsfield Street. Both men blamed the lights for the collision. Despite this, it would not be long before there were lights at most junctions in the city and many of them are probably still blamed for minor crashes to this day.

TERRIBLE TORSO

On 27 March 1793, at one o'clock in the afternoon, two men, James Lawlor and Denis Lyons, were taken from their cell at the city jail to Gallows Green and hanged. Gallows Green was the traditional site for public executions throughout the eighteenth century and early nineteenth century, although they would later be moved to the grounds of the prison.

This should have been the end of the story of Lawlor and Lyons but a few weeks later a dismembered torso washed up on the banks of the Shannon River. At first, this gruesome discovery was believed to be an act of murder but after some investigation it was discovered that the bodies of the two prisoners had been taken for dissection by one of the local surgeons. The persons later employed to inter the remains instead opted for a quicker disposal route and had thrown the torso into the river.

TWINNED TOWNS

The custom of twinning towns and sister cities is an attempt to foster communication, friendship and development between places throughout the world. Limerick city has several sister cities and, not surprisingly, these include a number in the United States as Ireland has a strong bond with its westerly neighbour.

The first of these special relationships with the United States became official on 4 March 1990, when the Mayor of Spokane, Washington State, signed the agreement with the Mayor of Limerick. A section of Bishop's Quay was renamed Spokane Walk after this twinning.

At the end of the decade another American sister joined the family; this time New Brunswick, New Jersey, in April 1999. The most recent addition to the Limerick/United States family is Santa Clara, California, which signed the agreement in July 2014.

There are two official connections with Ireland's easterly neighbour as well. These are with Birmingham, England, and Limerick Exiles Association, London. Continental relations are with Quimper, France, after whom Quimper Square in Cruise's Street is named, and Hohenlohekreis, Germany.

Three county villages are also involved in the twinning arrangements. These are Adare with Villecrenses, France, Murroe with Évry-Grégy, also France, and Ballylanders with Wyandotte County, Kansas City, USA. St Fintan's and St Joseph's schools in Doon have linked with Schlossgymnasium, Kunzelsau, Germany.

The Singer from Quimper sculpted by Rowan Gillespie in 1992, Quimper Square, Cruise's Street. (*Image courtesy of Liam O'Brien*)

U

UNUSUAL OCCUPATIONS

Trades have come and gone and what were once regular occupations would now seem very obscure. Every town and village once had a blacksmith, while weavers and basket makers were also common place. A wealthy man in the early 1700s would not be caught outside without his highly starched and curled white wig. The larger of these wigs, which trailed down the wearer's back, was known as a periwig, while the smaller version that sat on the top of the head was known as a peruke.

As the century rolled on, the larger wigs fell out of favour with all but magistrates. Meanwhile, the smaller perukes retained their popularity and in 1769, there were sixteen peruke makers in the city alone. As fashions changed, so did manufacturing. In 1846, when fashion dictated curled hair, John Egan with Thomas Street and William Woods on Mungret Street supplied the curls. Woods did not stay in the occupation long, being recorded as a feather merchant at his death two years later. Feathers were in hot demand for stuffing pillows at the time. The dapper man about town in 1877 would need to employ the services of Richard O'Neill, a 'looking glass maker' in Patrick Street.

Almost every Victorian man in Limerick City and County smoked a pipe. The cheapest and therefore the most common pipe used was made of clay. William Merritt operated the largest clay pipe factory in the city out of Broad Street, most of the employees consisting of family members. A standard pipe in the late nineteenth century cost a penny.

Those who were smoking clay pipes were unlikely to have been able to afford the service of the Tuite family. They were carriage trimmers, who in the 1870s and '80s would reupholster and decorate carriages in the latest styles. During that same period Michael O'Regan operated the strange combination of a postal service and funeral arrangers out of his premises on Cecil Street.

A century earlier, post was carried by horse-riding couriers known as postilions. One such postilion, Jeremiah Cusack, had his name in the papers in 1784. His former employer, C. Powell, was warning others not to employ him as he had run away from his position with no warning.

Occupations changed as Limerick entered the twentieth century. In 1901, Monaghan man William McClean was staying in Hartstonge Street, where he was employed as a colporteur, a person who distributes religious texts.

When telegrams were sent to the Jamaica Banana Agency at 3 Upper Denmark Street in the 1910s, the phrase 'Bananas, Limerick' was used. The Jamaica Banana Agency processed the green unripened bananas shipped in bulk to Limerick by placing them in rooms filled with ethylene gas, which ripened them ready for market.

Limerick-born James Victor and Anna Julia O'Connor were married in about 1897 in Scotland. The couple had five children, three of whom passed away when young in Lanarkshire. In 1911, they returned to Limerick to live with James' brother Thomas Patrick O'Connor.

What was unusual about this family were their occupations that year. The head of the household, James, was a scenic artist. His wife, brother and 13-year-old daughter Mary were all actors. The other two in the family were James' 10-year-old son James and 14-year-old nephew Frederick, both scholars.

The O'Connors shared a house in Nolan's Cottages with the Meaney family, headed by Patrick Meaney, who had the unusual occupation of 'time keeper' on the railway. He was responsible for making sure that trains left the station on time. Nolan's Cottages were located where the Limerick Council car park now stands behind City Hall.

In the earlier part of the nineteenth century the road to a lifelong career was a difficult one. At the time, apprentices in the form of indentured servants were common. This practice involved young men and women being tied to a master tradesman for a specified period, usually several years. During that time the apprentice would be taught a skill and the tradesman was required to provide food and lodgings. Many apprentices were also used as farm hands and domestic servants with little or no opportunity to escape from the serving class.

In 1812, the *Limerick Evening Post* printed notices from tradesmen about their apprentices. On 29 January 1812, George Hickey, a member of the Master Coopers of Ireland, warned other members of the guild against employing his former apprentice, Edmond Ryan. Ryan had left his apprenticeship two years earlier than agreed. Hickey also warned the public that he would prosecute anyone who was aiding Ryan. In the same notice he advertised for a new apprentice, one who was not a 'night walker' or prone to abscond.

A few days later, on 5 February 1812, James Regan of the Master Tailors of Limerick also had the same issue with an absconding apprentice, Samuel Monsell, who had left on 20 January and not returned.

UNEXPECTED VISITORS

The city was visited by three of the most famous boxers of the late twentieth century: George Foreman, Joe Frazier and Gene Tunney. Each had a very different experience during their time in Limerick.

In 1954, Tunney, the undefeated world heavy weight champion from 1926 to 1928, stopped in Limerick for dinner at the Brazen Head. He was on a tour of Ireland in an attempt to secure a writer to transform his autobiography, *A Man Must Fight*, into a film script. He signed autographs for all of those who recognised him in the city.

Frazier arrived as the headliner in a one-night only event in the City Theatre. The event was due to take place on 12 June 1970 and featured dancers from Las Vegas. However, Frazier was disappointed to see that only forty members of the public had turned up to the event. His disappointment turned into disgust and he refused to take the stage in front of such a small crowd.

In 1999, Foreman visited the Southill area of the city. He was so overwhelmed by the reception he received that he donated $60,000 to be split evenly between Southill Marching Band, the Southill Boxing Club and Fr Joe Young's soccer academy.

On 13 March 1965, Limerick greeted a very unusual visitor, Che Guevara. The Cuban revolutionary was on board a plane from Prague to Havana when it was forced to land in Shannon due to engine trouble. While waiting for the plane to be repaired, Guevara and some friends visited Limerick for a night of revelry. They stopped into the Hanratty Hotel on Glentworth Street, where pints flowed freely. The following morning Guevara returned to Shannon Airport bedecked in sprigs of shamrock, as it was St Patrick's week.

On 19 June 1961, Prince Ranier III of Monaco, his wife the actress Grace Kelly and their children passed through Limerick city on their way to Adare. Even though the royal couple did not stop in the city, the streets were still lined with crowds. Almost all the stores closed after lunch as the female staff left their posts to find the best vantage point. At four o'clock in the evening they passed

On Wednesday September 1 1897, the Duke of York George Frederick Ernest Albert, the future King George V left Adare Manor. (*Image courtesy of the National Library of Ireland*)

through O'Connell Street to loud cheers and waves from the gathered mass vying for a glimpse of the famous couple.

When the cavalcade reached Adare, they were greeted by hundreds of locals clapping and cheering. The royal family were guests of Lord and Lady Dunraven. They were to attend a dinner at Kilgobbin before spending the night in the Dunraven Arms Hotel. The following morning, the family left Adare for Parknasilla, Kerry.

Fourteen years later, Limerick was touched once more by Princess Grace. In September that year her secretary, Louisette Levy-Soussan, wrote to the director of the City Theatre, Jack Bourke, on behalf of the princess. She wished to thank him for attempting to revive theatre in the city. A cheque for $250 signed by the princess was enclosed in the letter.

UP, UP AND AWAY

In 1785 the first hot-air balloon flight took place in Ireland, only fourteen months after the first flight in the world. The balloonist was Wicklow man Richard Crosbie, who flew across Dublin. The following April, Crosbie arrived in Limerick with his balloon.

He set up his marvellous contraption on the North Strand (Clancy Strand). At noon on 27 April 1786, he began to inflate it. He stopped when he began to run low on the gas, which began producing sulfuric acid. Runners were sent out in all directions, but a new supply could not be found in the city centre and Crosbie decided to continue with the little gas he had left.

As he drifted up over the city, he looked out at the majestic Shannon River with its little islands forming a beautiful sight. Crosbie attempted to draw the scene, but his talents were not as an artist. However, his balloon was captured for John Ferrar's 1787 publication *History of Limerick*. The publication includes an engraving of it drifting over Limerick City.

The balloon rose higher as he drifted down the estuary towards Tarbert. He soon found himself hovering over a small green field in Limerick County for a half an hour. He took that opportunity to eat dinner and drink a bottle of wine, in what may have been the first instance of drink flying in the country.

He was soon off again. The balloon rose higher and Crosbie began to feel the effects of the cold, so he descended into a lower altitude. The wind had turned and now the balloon was being pushed back towards Limerick city. After spending six hours in the sky, the adventurer decided it was time to land. He had hoped to return to his departure point, but the wind decided otherwise for him.

He landed in a field in near where Shannon Airport is today and hurried to secure the balloon and basket. He spotted two locals and called for assistance, but they fled from the strange sight before them. The wind continued to carry the balloon forward until he reached a wall, where Crosbie began throwing stones into the basket to weigh it down. Unfortunately, his efforts were in vain as the wall collapsed and his basket ascended without him. The balloon was located by Captain O'Brien in Ennis and returned to its owner.

It would be more than sixty years before another balloon was seen in the skies over Limerick. It was the height of the famine when John Hampton climbed into the basket of one named Erin go Bragh. The time was coming up to five o'clock in the evening on 3 September 1849 and a crowd had gathered at James Marshall's Repository on Upper Cecil Street to look in awe at this wondrous sight.

Unlike Crosbie, Hampton was not alone in the floating carriage. The basket could carry six but for this flight there were only two other passengers: Hampden Russell, a banker, and Mr Townsend, a civil engineer. There were grumblings prior to take off as two other men, Henry Vereker and an Excise officer, attempted to board even though they had not booked a place. On his previous journeys Hampton had been accompanied by his wife but on this occasion she gave up her seat to sandbags.

Marshall's Repository had been a hive of activity in the days leading up to the flight. Three large platforms with seating were constructed around the departure point. A band from the barracks entertained the crowd before lift-off. The prices for reserved seating with the best vantage point was 2*s*. Second-tier seating was 1*s* and children were admitted for 6*d*. All those in the surrounding area could witness the flight for free once it cleared the roofs and more did that than those who paid for the spectacle.

As the balloon rose, the band played the national anthem. The wind took it down towards the Shannon River, which they crossed. Here they hovered for several minutes admiring the cityscape spread out before them. Russell described the scene as that of a miniature model. He stated that Lough Derg could be seen from that vantage point.

They were soon on the move again, crossing the Clare border and finding themselves over the mass expanse of trees of Cratloe Woods. It was at this point

An aerial view of The King's Island as it would appear if gliding over it in a hot-air balloon. (*Image courtesy of Donal Stundon*)

that Hampton used the barometer provided by Richard Wallace, owner of the observatory.

They followed the river again, finding themselves above the bank opposite the mouth of the Maigue River. Russell took note of the silence, removed as they were from the usual earthly sounds. The wind changed, and the three men found themselves travelling rapidly in the direction of Ennis. Hampton prepared for the descent and the basket hit the ground outside Newmarket-on-Fergus.

They were soon surrounded by locals offering aid to gather up the balloon. Mr Creagh, of Ralahine, offered his horse and cart to transport the balloon back to the city. Three weeks later Hampton delivered a lecture at the Theatre Royal, Henry Street. Sadly, this talk on the 'science and progress of Aerostation' was very poorly attended and Hampton never recouped the cost of his flight in Limerick.

Balloonists Gwen Bellew and Martin Moroney arrived in Limerick from London to recreate Crosbie's inaugural flight in Limerick. They ascended from Clancy Strand on 12 September 1970. Large crowds gathered on the beautiful blue-skied day to watch as the balloon floated across the city to Caherconlish, a flight that lasted just under fifty minutes.

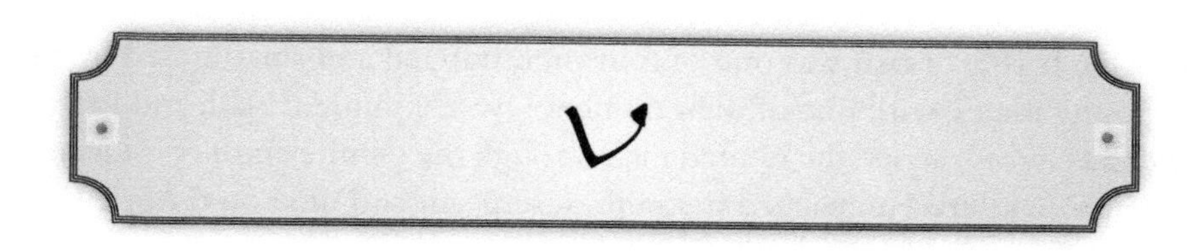

THE VICTORIA CROSS

The Victoria Cross was established in 1856. It is given to members of the British armed forces who show extraordinary courage in the face of hostile forces. Several Limerick men received this rare honour while serving.

Joseph Bradshaw was born in 1835 in Dromkeen and was a private in the Rifle Brigade during the Crimean War. He received his Victoria Cross for his actions on 22 April 1855, when he and Private Robert Humpston attacked and captured a Russian rifle pit. Securing this area was of utmost importance to the campaign and he was promoted to the rank of corporal. He attended Hyde Park in 26 June 1857 and was among the first to receive the medal. The ceremony was conducted by Queen Victoria herself.

Also receiving the award that day was William Coffey. Coffey was born on 5 August 1829 in Knocklong and, like Bradshaw, he was a private serving during the Crimean war. While squashed into a trench with his comrades on 29 March 1855, Coffey spotted a live shell had fallen in. He quickly threw it over the parapet, saving the lives of everyone who surrounded him. He later achieved the rank of sergeant. He passed away on 13 July 1875 in Chesterfield, England.

John Crimmin was born on 19 March 1859 in Bruff. He trained as a physician. When 29 years old, he was serving as a surgeon in the Indian Army, and received the Victoria Cross for his action on New Year's Day 1889. He was on duty in Burma when a lieutenant and four soldiers charged into enemy fire. As the battle raged, Crimmin tended the wounds of two of the men before assisting in driving back the attacking force.

As he returned to attend the wounded he was attacked several times, continually being forced to fend the enemy off with his sword. He was later raised to the rank of colonel. He died on 20 February 1945 in Somerset.

William Nash was born on 23 April 1824 in Newcastle West and was a corporal in the Rifle Brigade when his valiant action took place in India. On 11 March 1858, Nash was one of four men trapped and surrounded by the opposing forces, with one of their number severely injured. Nash and Private David Hawkes carried the injured man through the gunfire and a considerable distance to safety. He reached the rank of sergeant and died on 6 April 1875 in Middlesex, England.

The wonderfully named Nathaniel Godolphin Burslem was born in Limerick on 2 February 1837. Burslem quickly followed in his father's footsteps by enlisting in the army and became a lieutenant stationed in China. On 21 August 1860, he and Private Thomas Lane swam through ditches to breach the wall of a fort to allow his comrades to enter. They succeeded in their attempt but were both severely wounded in the process. He left the army and travelled to New Zealand, where he drowned in an accident on 14 July 1865.

John Danaher was born on 25 June 1860 in Limerick city and when he was 20 he joined the Connaught Rangers. He was very quickly on the frontline in South Africa during the First Boer War. On 16 January 1881 he and fellow Connaught Ranger James Murray rescued a severely wounded private while under heavy fire. Danaher was presented with his Victoria Cross on 23 August 1882 by Viceroy Curragh in Ireland. He retired from the army and opened a public house in Portsmouth, where he died on 9 January 1919.

Michael James O'Rourke was born in Limerick in 1878 but immigrated to Canada before the First World War. He was a naturalised Canadian citizen when he received the Victoria Cross for his action in August 1917. During that time, he was a private and a stretcher bearer for the Canadian Expeditionary Force. For three days he worked nonstop bringing the wounded from the battlefield under heavy machine-gun fire. Dressing their wounds and feeding them, he undoubtedly saved countless lives. He died on 6 December 1957 in Vancouver, Canada. This made him the most recent Limerick recipient of the Victoria Cross.

VIANELLO OF VENICE

In October 1849, the *Paolino* of Venice and the *Sano Fratelli* set sail from the city. The ships anchored at Grass Island, where seven men from the two ships took to a smaller boat to attend Mass at Ballybrown Chapel. Among the men were two Italians, Captain A. Vianello of the *Paolina* and his brother Francisco

Vianello, as well as Captain Geovanni Antonio Descovish of the *Sano Fratelli*. Also on board were George Hewson, who acted as a translator for the visitors, and local man John Greene of Greene Island.

The boat was being piloted up the Maigue River by Greene. The Greene family were river pilots who had lived on Greene Island for generations and would guide larger vessels up the Maigue and Shannon rivers.

Unfortunately, the boat ran on to one of the mud banks that are prevalent in the area. It became stuck and needed the assistance of a ship to pull her out. As there was no precision in the sails, once the boat was released from the mud it capsized, tipping all eight men into the strong current. Hewson held on to the boat for as long as he could until all attempts at rescuing him failed. He swam nearly a quarter of a mile to shore. Four other men used the same tactic but sadly three of them, including the Vianello brothers, perished under the water. George Hewson continued to act as an interpreter in Limerick until his death thirteen years later.

VICIOUS VIKINGS

The monastery in Mungret was founded by Saint Nessan prior to in the mid-sixth century. The monastery at one point encompassed six churches and was home to up to 1500 monks and the auxiliary labourers and their families. It was one of the richest locations on the west coast of Ireland and as such was a prime target for marauding Vikings.

St Mary's Roman Catholic Church on Athlunkard Street. The name is derived from Irish Áth Longphuirt (the Ford of the Longphort) and is a nod to Limerick's Viking past. (*Author's collection*)

Mungret monastery was plundered by the Vikings four times during the ninth century. In 835, the community was burnt by the raiders from the sea. The Vikings had settled in Limerick city by the early tenth century and lived peacefully there.

Meanwhile, the monastery at Mungret was not left in peace; it was burnt in 1088 by Ulsterman Domhnall Mac Lochlain, and in 1107 it was plundered by local chief Murtagh O Brien. Despite this, Mungret continued as a centre of religious life in Ireland for centuries, though changing denominations over time.

Traces of the Vikings can still be seen today through place names such as the Lax Weir, lax being the Danish word for salmon.

THE VON TRAPP FAMILY

The O'Mara family were most famous for their bacon factory and the opera singer Joseph O'Mara. Joseph was the second youngest of James O'Mara and Hanora Foley's thirteen children. As a boy, he sang in the choirs at St John's Cathedral and St Michael's Church. He trained in Milan and was the principal tenor at the Theatre Royal, Drury Lane, London, for three years. He was given the Freedom of Limerick on 2 October 1908. In 1912, he founded O'Mara's Travelling Opera Company. In 1926, he was the first tenor to be broadcast on the new Irish radio station.

The O'Mara bacon factory's offices in London were run by James junior. Sadly, James junior and his wife, Mysie McKenna, passed away only a few short years after their marriage. They left two orphaned daughters, 7-year-old Constance 'Connie' and Hanora 'Daisy', to be raised between families and boarding schools.

In 1913, as a young woman, Connie travelled to Vienna, Austria, to work as a governess. She quickly met and became engaged to Baron Werner von Trapp, who was nine years older than her. Baron Werner von Trapp also happened to be the brother of Georg Ritter von Trapp of the world famous von Trapp family singers.

Connie became Baroness von Trapp when the pair married on 9 June 1914 at the Chapel Hoyos, Fiume, in the Austro-Hungarian Empire. Their daughter, also named Connie, was born within the year. Sadly, this was during the First World War and her husband was killed in action on 2 May 1915. Connie was left a young mother, widowed and parentless in a new country, while still in her early twenties.

Georg Ritter von Trapp named his son Werner in honour of his brother. This son was portrayed as Kurt in *The Sound of Music.* Connie and her daughter lived with her in-laws until the von Trapps fled Austria in 1938. Connie remained behind and was remarried in 1941 to Count Johann Heribert, when she gained the title of Countess.

Connie would visit Limerick on several occasions while she was Baroness von Trapp and Countess Herberstein. It is not known if her daughter inherited the von Trapp singing gene. She died on 24 March 1952 in Hartberg, Austria. Her sister Daisy returned to Limerick and was living at Auburn Villas, O'Connell Avenue, when she married Dr William J. O'Sullivan on 27 November 1914, in St Joseph's Church.

THE VIRTUAL VOICE

Long before sound was included in motion pictures, a Limerick man, Frank Goggin, brought the stories to life. Goggin lived at Fogerty's Range and worked as a stage manager in the Theatre Royal, Henry Street. The early motion pictures would be shown with a live musical accompaniment and the dialogue would appear in a new frame.

There were many in the audience in the early years who were illiterate, so often missed essential plot points. Goggin decided that this would not do. He placed himself behind the screen and not only read the dialogue cards but added his own sound effects into the scenes. It would have been highly amusing to hear romantic leads professing their love in strong Limerick accents. Sadly, the Theatre Royal was destroyed in a fire in 1922 and Goggin's voice acting came to an end.

Drawing of the Theatre Royal before it was destroyed in a fire in the 1920s. (*Image courtesy of Limerick Leader*)

THE WINDMILL OF WINDMILL STREET

Standing on the northern bank of the Shannon River and looking towards Limerick City in the late eighteenth century was reminiscent of Holland. There were three windmills visible at the time: one on the Ennis Road, which was dismantled in 1811; one at Ballinacurra, which stood over 50ft high; and the third stood at the bank of the river at the end of the aptly named Windmill Street.

At the time, Edmund Sexton Pery's new town was under construction and his brother-in-law, Lancelot Hill, took advantage of the development. Hill erected a picture postcard windmill, a large round stone building that tapered inwards at the top. On 29 January 1803, the windmill hit the headlines for the first time as it caught fire. Luckily, this caused only slight damage and the machinery was back in action quickly.

In 1810, Hill passed away aged 76. The next owner was Laurence Durack. Only three years later, under Durack's watch, the windmill became the site of an incredible drama. On 13 August 1813, a crowd gathered beneath the sails of the windmill, having arrived to witness a duel.

The men bearing arms that day were Maurice Magrath and Daniel O'Connell. This was the Daniel O'Connell who would later become known as The Liberator and after whom O'Connell Street was named. The men's dispute began a day earlier when Magrath threw a book at O'Connell's head while they were both in court. This act was in retaliation for O'Connell calling Magrath a liar.

Having a projectile thrust towards him infuriated O'Connell. He sought counsel with his friend, Nicholas Purcell O'Gorman, and quickly challenged Magrath to a duel. The place and time were set, and both men arrived with their entourage at the field next to the windmill.

The windmill on Windmill Street prior to 1916. (*Image Limerick Museum*)

Mr O'Gorman, who assisted O'Connell, and Mr Bennett, who assisted Magrath, measured the points at which both men should stand. After taking up their positions, and with a pistol in his hand, Magrath apologised for his actions the previous day but O'Connell was slow to accept it. He was counselled by his friends in attendance until agreement was reached. Both men, with pistols still at the ready, advanced to each other and shook hands. The duellists both returned to the city in the same carriage and the excitement of the day was over.

Only a few short months after the aborted duel the windmill saw its most dramatic event. On the night of 15 November 1813, the entire building was engulfed in flames. The machinery was still in motion as the sails burned, leaving a beautiful, yet tragic, trail in the sky. Fortuitously, the windmill owner, Durack, had an insurance policy. A year and a half later he received a very large pay-out of over £1,339, which would equate to over a million euros today. As for the windmill, it sat undisturbed for just over a hundred years before being dismantled and the stones used as ship ballast.

A WEIRD WEDDING TRADITION

In July 1864, the wedding of Cornelius McMahon and Bridget William took place at St Mary's Chapel, Athlunkard Street. The couple were both widowed, and the groom claimed to be 50 years old on his marriage certificate, although another report would show him to be a 75-year-old great grandfather. His bride was no spring chicken, claiming to be a 46 and the daughter of a rag and bone collector. The entire wedding party was illiterate, and this may account for the disparity in recorded ages.

As the newlyweds left the church, a large group from the neighbourhood gathered to wish them well. The crowd were quite boisterous, using stones in cans and kettles to create an enormous racket. This was the traditional way to greet older couples on their wedding day in the parish.

A local police constable, Cronin, did not approve of these antics and insisted that the crowd be quieted down. When they refused, he arrested the ringleaders, a girl called Mary Gloster and an old woman Ellen Mullins, also known as Mary.

During the subsequent trial, Mullins insisted that if a crowd had not gathered and created such a ruckus the couple would have been highly disappointed. When asked, the constable confirmed that it was a tradition in the area. Mayor Eugene O'Callaghan dismissed the case, gave Mullins back her kettle and told her to do no harm the next time there was a wedding in the parish.

Although the case of a crowd giving a bridal couple a noisy send-off had a happy ending, not all wedding traditions were as pleasant or well received. In the early part of the nineteenth century the act of abduction was not a rare occurrence. An abduction was the act of kidnapping an unmarried woman, usually of means, which would sully her reputation if she was not returned within a few hours. To avoid shame on her household, the abductor was often permitted to marry his victim. Luckily, most abduction attempts failed.

On 14 November 1847, the Molony family of Croagh was struck by one of these attacks. Roger Molony and his wife were enjoying a quiet evening by the fire, while most of their children were in bed, when their solitude was suddenly interrupted by a gang bearing guns rushing into the house. The gang was made up of Michael Madigan, Patrick Gleeson, Thomas Frawley, Jeremiah Garvan and the Looney brothers, Michael and Daniel.

The house was filled with commotion as Roger and his son John were locked in cupboards and shots were fired. Upstairs, Kate Molony sought solace in her sister Mary's bed. She was spotted by Michael Looney, who was making his way up the stairs. He and several of the other men grabbed her and began dragging Kate down the stairs. In the process, Kate attempted to escape, breaking the banister in her struggle.

The gang carried Kate out the door while she was still in her nightdress. She was carried through wet and boggy fields for about a mile until they reached John Farrell's house. Here the gang allowed Kate to take a drink of water before moving on again.

Soon they stopped at Richard Creagh's house. They told Kate to wait there as they were going to find a priest to marry her to Michael Looney. Richard Creagh's wife was having no part in this kidnapping and pulled Kate away. She gave her clean clothes and a bed to sleep on.

At the same time, Kate's family had raised the alarm and soon four of the gang were caught. They were in Rathkeale attempting to find a priest. Patrick Gleeson and Michael Looney evaded capture for a few days but were finally caught as they exited a coach arriving in Cork from Charleville.

Kate was returned to her family the following morning. In January 1848, the trial of the gang took place in Limerick. Strangely, Kate pleaded for clemency for Michael Looney, who had carried her through the bog. This call worked in his favour as he received a sentence of twelve months in prison while the rest of the gang were transported to Australia for fourteen years.

WIDOWS ALMS HOME

Although the Widows Alms Houses on Nicholas Street bear the inscription 'Corporation Widows Alms Houses A.D. 1691', they were in fact constructed over a century and a half later. The site of the Alms Houses was previously that of St Nicholas Church. This church was sacked after the 1691 Williamite Siege of Limerick. Although it was no longer in use, the building remained until the early 1700s.

Soon after this the Corporation constructed a building for the care of twenty widows. By the 1840s this building was in a ruinous state and there was a call to have it replaced. In 1848, John Duggan, a major building contractor in Pery Street, won the contract for the new building. Also, in the 1840s, he was responsible for the construction of Mathew Bridge, for extensions to the workhouse and for flagging (re-paving) the Milk Market.

Despite having a contract for the building, Duggan had to pay for materials up front, as the Corporation were slow to pay. This caused Duggan to go into debt with the building supplier Francis Spaight. Spaight forced the Corporation to issue a security bond to Duggan and the work continued. This debt would remain until after Duggan's death on 25 March 1849, when Spaight took a claim out of the estate.

Meanwhile, in August 1848, the newly constructed Widows Alms Houses were furnished and the first occupants moved in. In November 1849, the widows received a welcome treat after two women were arrested for stealing geese near Plassey. The women were sent to jail and the geese to the widows in the Alms Houses. They were also supplied with a substantial Christmas dinner by the mayor that year.

It was not all roses in the Alms Houses as there was no sewer connected to the building until 1856 and it would take over a century for the houses to gain indoor plumbing and electricity. In 1962, Bridget Riordan, who was 93 years old, used oil lamps to light her small apartment and collected water from the tap outside.

This news led to an outcry among the local community, who set up a fund to connect the houses to the electrical grid. One of the schemes run by the locals was in Michael Crowe's public house; he put an extra penny on each pint towards the fund. Soon the community raised enough so the widows could have access to instant lighting, although indoor toilets were still a few years away. Bridget O'Riordan remained in the Alms Houses until her death on 25 February 1969, when she was nearly 100 years old.

As the twentieth century neared its end and the widows slowly passed away, their rooms were not reoccupied. The building was boarded up until it became the headquarters of St Mary's Aid in 2009.

WALKING ON WATER

Sitting as it does on the west coast of Ireland, Limerick is often hit by wild winds and storms coming in from the Atlantic Ocean. The poet William Wordsworth remarked on visiting Limerick in 1829, 'it is raining hard now, and has done so all day'. Almost every year a storm will bring about damage in the city and county, but the following are some of the most destructive in modern history.

First are records of a violent wind storm that hit the city on 30 July 1696. The wind blew with such intensity for three hours that it turned back the tide in the Shannon River. This allowed people to traverse the waterway without wetting their feet. Although an amusing scene, the storm brought with it a continued drain on the economy as the fields due to be harvested were damaged irrevocably and the price of wheat and barley increased exponentially.

The reverse effect transpired almost fifty years later, when a storm caused the Shannon River to rise so high that four ships were swept on to the quay. The water rose to a level that it covered the floor of the newly built St Mary's Chapel on Athlunkard Street in 2ft of water. Meanwhile in the county, livestock and hay were caught in the wind and moved some distance.

A severe frost began on 3 November 1683, which lasted until 9 February 1684. It caused an ice plate on the Shannon that, according to John Ferrar in his history of Limerick, was 7 or 8ft thick. It was sturdy enough that carriages and cattle frequently crossed the river from King's Island to Parteen. This severe frost was superseded in 1739, the year of the great frost. This lasted forty days and brought about a famine.

WOEFUL WITCHCRAFT

In 1865, Michael Roche married Bridget Collins in St John's Cathedral, but their marriage was not a happy one. Three years after the wedding, Bridget's brothers', John and Michael Collins, were up in court after assaulting Roche. The brothers did not approve of Roche's drinking and how he was treating their sister. They claimed he was spending all the money he earned as a tobacco spinner on alcohol, leaving them to support Bridget and her children.

Since it was Michael who caused Roche physical harm by hitting him with a poker, he was fined 10*s*, while John was freed without charge. That was not the end of the tribulations at the trial as also in the court that day was Roche's father and the mother of the Collins family.

The most famous trial to take place in the old city courthouse was for the murder of the Colleen Bawn. (*Author's collection*)

The matriarch of the Collins family cursed at the patriarch of the Roche family, also named Michael, throughout the proceedings, claiming that he was responsible for the ill treatment of her daughter at the hands of his son. The mother threw herself on her knees in front of the old man, praying that God would strike him down. The father left the court in a hurry but as he crossed the doorstep he collapsed and his body contorted violently.

A crowd outside the court ran to the woman who instigated the curse and begged her to lift it, but she refused even when compelled to do so by the police. The ailing man was transported to Barrington's Hospital, George's Quay, where Dr McMahon diagnosed that Roche had suffered a stroke. He was then taken to the workhouse hospital to convalesce, where he passed away before the end of the year.

As for old Mrs Collins, after this the people in her neighbourhood looked at her with fear. This caused them to give her gifts to avoid receiving the wrath of her tongue.

X

X MARKS THE SPOT

In 1854 a mine was opened in Oola on the Limerick Tipperary border by the Oola Silver, Lead and Copper Mining Company. It was a subscription-based company, with 12,000 subscribers paying £1 each.

The subscribers were wooed by the claim that the area was highly mineralised. It did not faze them that a previous mine on the site had closed

One of the bore holes for sampling land in the Oola Hills for precious metals. (*Image courtesy of* Limerick Leader)

only seven years earlier. Luckily for the subscribers, their wager paid off and the mine in Oola stayed open until the 1890s. After the closure of the mine, the enormous iron waterwheel was sold to another mining company in Aberystwyth, Wales.

The mine sat idle for over sixty years until a Canadian mining company arrived at Michael O'Grady's farm in July 1962. They were hoping to get rich by striking a seam of precious metal. There were officials from the Department of Industry and Commerce on the site and in the surrounding Oola Hills surveying the land under the Mineral Development Acts of 1940 and 1960. Luckily for the environment, but sadly for the company's finances and local economy, X did not mark the spot and no bands of ore were unearthed.

When Brigadier Sean Wall concealed two rifles in the ceiling of a room in St Joseph's Hospital during the Irish War of Independence he probably never imagined that it would take over thirty years for the gun to be touched by another human hand. One of the rifles was constructed from a 1913 German design, while the other was much older.

Wall was born in Bruff in 1888. He was a member of the East Limerick Brigade of the IRA and fought in the Irish War of Independence. When staying in Limerick city, Wall was known to take refuge in St Joseph's Hospital. It is presumed that in 1921, he stashed the guns there not long before he was killed in action in East Tipperary. This would explain why they remained undiscovered until October 1954, when Daniel Moore carried out building works at the hospital.

On 12 October 1952, a memorial to Wall was erected in his home town of Bruff, and was unveiled by the President of Ireland, Sean T. O'Ceallaigh. The memorial also commemorates five other members of the East Limerick Brigade who were killed in action at Caherguillamore on 27 December 1920.

XAVIER IS THE NAME

Mary Elizabeth Mackey, the sister of fishing expert Anthony Mackey, of Castleconnell, joined the Presentation sisters as a young woman. In 1873, before she took her vows she set sail to Australia on board the SS *Great Britain* with a little band of pioneer sisters destined for Melbourne. All seven who travelled, Mother Paul Mulquin, Sisters Mary Berchmans Carroll, Margaret Mary Cronin, Bernard Gunson, Patrick Irwin, and fellow aspirant Anne Bray, were from Limerick.

The sisters quickly established Windsor Convent, the first Presentation convent in Australia. Their doors opened as a school the following year. In 1876, Mackey took her vows and became Sister Mary Xavier, named after St Francis Xavier, patron saint of Australia. She rose to the rank of Mother Superior and was passionate about education, especially science and art.

An 1876 image of the Limerick sisters who set up the first Presentation convent in Australia. From left to right: Sr Margaret Mary Cronin, Fr James Corbett, Mother Paul Mulquin, Sr Berchmans Carroll, Sr Patrick Irwin, Sr Xavier Mackey, Sr Joseph Kennedy, Sr Bernard Gunson, Sr Monica Bray. (*Image courtesy of Windsor Convent*)

Nearly fifty years later she returned to Limerick, where she succeeded in persuading several postulants to travel to Australia to carry out their missionary work. In 1923, an envoy of Mother Xavier, travelling with twenty young women from Limerick, went to her new home in Australia.

In 1936, Mother Xavier celebrated her diamond jubilee with the Windsor Convent. She passed away in 1940 and over fifty priests attended her funeral. The convent school founded by these Limerick women announced its closure in 2020.

Another Limerick woman founded a convent on another continent. Mary Walsh was born in London to Limerick parents. Following their death when she was only 3 years old, her paternal grandmother travelled to collect her and raised her in the parish of Knockaderry. She attended the National School in Castlemahon and the St Catherine's Convent school in Newcastle West.

On the death of her grandmother, when she was only 18 years old, she set sail for the United States to a grand uncle who was residing in Pennsylvania. She quickly relocated herself to New York, where she worked as a servant.

In 1879, while working in wealthy homes, she was touched by the poverty and resulting ill-health that she saw in her own neighbourhood in New York. This moved her to found the Dominican Sisters of the Sick Poor. In 1910, her order was officially recognised by the Catholic Church. She passed away in 1922.

YOBBISH YOUTHS

Constable Hardy brought before the Limerick Petty Sessions of 15 March 1844 a 'thimble rigger' named Swift. He was swift by name and nature as through sleight of hand he pickpocketed several countrymen outside the courthouse as they gathered to attend the Limerick County Assize. He was convicted and immediately sent to jail.

That same day an unnamed young boy, who gained his wage as a pigeon trapper, was ordered to return a tumbler that he had stolen from Alexander Winiss, Royal Horse Artillery. Also, two corn brokers, Patrick Burns and Thomas Downes, were fined £2 10*s* for filling the bottom of their bags with lead with the purpose of overcharging the customers.

In October 1867, Joseph Matterson, owner of the famous bacon factory, noticed that he was frequently missing money and could not figure out where it was going. Meanwhile, one of his employees, Joseph Connolly, a young lad of 16, began purchasing expensive pipes and cigars. Matterson realised that he was not paying this boy enough for him to afford these luxuries, so, to catch the thief, he marked a half sovereign and two florins and placed them in the usual spot in a locked cabinet. Connolly then ingeniously used a bent rod to retrieve the coins through the bottom of the cabinet. Caught, Connolly admitted his guilt and was sentenced to three months in prison.

The adventures of a 10-year-old Limerick boy stretched all the way to New York. In 1890, young Timothy Walters was the eldest surviving child of a Thomondgate family. His two older brothers had passed away aged 6 and 10 only a few years earlier. With this history, Timothy did not want to become a burden on his family and he plotted his escape. He made his way to what was then Queenstown (now Cobh) where emigrant ships sailed daily.

There he snuck on board the *City of Rome* destined for New York. He avoided the ticket collector by hiding himself away and once the tickets were collected he was free to roam the ship with the other steerage passengers.

When the ship docked in New York, young Tim clung to the skirts of a second-class passenger and was assumed to be her child, so he was not stopped by anyone. With only 30 cents in his pocket the enterprising young lad took himself to the Labour Bureau, where he was given immediate employment at St Omer Hotel.

Meanwhile, his parents in Limerick were searching for their missing son. He remained undetected for two weeks, when he was caught stealing lumps of sugar. He was then removed to Father Drumgoole's asylum in Staten Island before being returned to Ireland.

THE YEILDING FAMILY

In 1850, an unusual redaction was placed in the *Limerick Chronicle* after it had mistakenly announced the death of Mrs Margaret Yeilding, the wife of Hugo Eldon Yeilding, and their relation Miss Mary Frances Yeilding, the only daughter of William Richard Yeilding, both of Glenstar Lodge. The Glenstar Lodge was situated in the main Newcastle West to Carrigkerry road. Some unknown persons using the signature of Mary Yeilding had sent the false information into the newspaper. Despite the malice against her, Mrs Margaret survived for another fifty-six years.

The Yeilding family owned cotton factories in England and India and became landlords in the district known as Glensharrold. The Yeildings proved to be very fair landlords and many tenants who lived in smallholdings had no rent to pay during the harsh famine period. Due in part to this kindness, the Yeilding family later became bankrupt.

In 1853 the land of Glensharrold was bought by Christopher Delmage, who had married into the Yeilding family but did not have their sensibility when it came to tenants and was extremely disliked among them. In the late 1880s the family pushed for large-scale evictions on the estate despite the opposition of the Roman Catholic Bishop of Limerick and several Members of Parliament.

The women of the 1880s were not just standing idly by as men formed the Land League to protect tenant farmers from eviction. The Ladies' Land League was founded by Anna and Fanny Parnell, the sisters of Charles Stewart Parnell, one of the founders of the Land League.

The Limerick branch of the Ladies' Land League was active from 1881, attending the auctions of seized farms along with its male counterpart.

The League became headline news in Limerick on 21 April 1882. That day Judge Clifford Lloyd sentenced Dublin League member Anne Kirk to three months imprisonment in Limerick after she convinced the tenants in the district of Tulla, Co. Clare to not pay their rents. The judge offered leniency with the option of bail with the requirement that she keep the peace; 24-year-old Kirk refused.

During her time in prison she was allowed outside of her dark and gloomy cell for two hours a day and had visitors daily. The visitor who spoke to Kirk through the bars of her cell reported her treatment to the press each day.

A month later she was joined in Limerick female prison by fellow league member Mary Gleeson. Gleeson had been arrested in Nenagh for writing letters to tenants encouraging them not to pay rents. Just like Kirk, Gleeson was offered leniency but chose prison. She was taken by train from Nenagh to Limerick. She was accompanied to the train by the Nenagh Brass Band playing 'God Save Ireland'.

On 5 June 1882, both women were released from prison early and unconditionally due to a mass release order by the Lord Lieutenant of Ireland. They both received congratulations from the Limerick branch of the League before departing the city that evening.

The Yeilding ladies were not the only premature death report in the *Limerick Chronicle*. On 16 July 1885, the paper announced the death of Dr Jonathan Elmes. This came a surprise to the doctor as, although he had suffered from a seizure in his home on Thomas Street, he was still very much alive. The newspaper printed a retraction, blaming the mistake on a rumour that was circling around the city. He would actually pass away on 16 November 1893, aged 79. Once again the *Limerick Chronicle* would publish his death notice. He was the brother of Rev. John Elmes, the curate of St John's Church, whose headline story is told in the Desecration of the Dead section.

HOMES OF YESTERYEAR

The streetscape of Limerick city was very different in the mid-eighteenth century. Thousands of people were crammed into Englishtown and Irishtown, where space came at a premium. Even the bridge crossing the Abbey River connecting these two sections of the city was lined on both sides by buildings.

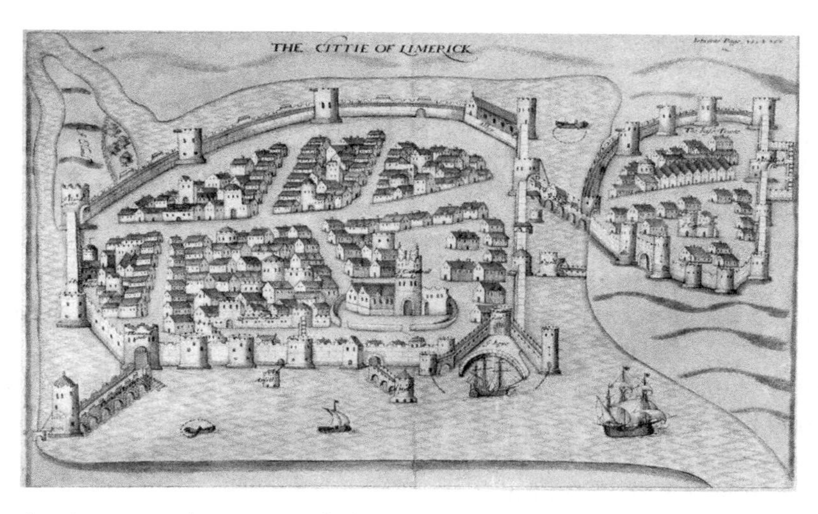

Map showing sixteenth century walled Limerick with houses on Baal's Bridge connecting the Irishtown and Englishtown. (*Image courtesy of the Limerick Museum*)

In 1769, the buildings had businesses on the ground floor and residential apartments above them. That year, the businesses on the street included tobacconists, card makers, haberdashers, silversmiths and whip makers. One of the occupants, George Bell, was a Master in the Freemason Lodge.

On 4 February 1775, Mr Berry was sitting quietly at his home on Baal's Bridge when the floor gave way beneath him. He plunged straight down into the Abbey River, where he was swept by the current towards the Shannon River. He was in luck that John Fitzgerald, a sailor, watched the strange event and came to Berry's rescue.

The old bridge was replaced in 1831, by the bridge that still stands today. This bridge was designed by the Pain Brothers. While this new bridge was being erected, a brass Masonic square inscribed with the date 1507 was discovered. On one side of the square are the words, 'I will strive to live with love and care', while the reverse reads 'upon the level and by the square'.

THE YOUNGEST SOLDIER

John Nash was the eldest of Jane Kett and Martin Nash's children. He was born on 21 February 1900 in Humphrey's Lane, off John Street. The family moved often between houses in the John Street area. His father, a labourer, passed away from tuberculosis when John was only 13 years old. This caused

Nash to grow up quickly. He was a member of the Limerick City regiment of the Irish Volunteers.

As the First World War broke out, Nash signed up for the 2nd Battalion of the Royal Munster Fusiliers, where he sought a young man's escapade, but was also a means of gaining a guaranteed wage to help support his mother and younger siblings. Sadly, his adventure was tragically cut short as he entered the realities of war. Despite his young age, Nash was a lance corporal when he went in to battle in France on 27 February 1916, just six days after his sixteenth birthday.

On the following day Chaplain George Craven wrote to Nash's widowed mother back in Limerick. He told of how Nash was brought into his hospital severely wounded the day before. Craven immediately gave him the last Sacraments and prepared him for death. Nash passed away the following morning from his wounds and Craven buried him alongside his comrades at Bethune Town Cemetery, Pas-de-Calais, France. The chaplain remarked that there is 'consolation for you at the feet of Our Lord crucified and the thought of your Boy's Christian death. Your loss is His gain for, please God he will soon be in Heaven.' This letter was published in the *Limerick Leader* two weeks later.

Nash was undoubtedly the youngest Limerick soldier killed in action during the First World War. He was only one of over a thousand Limerick citizens who died in the conflict. His mother, Jane never, remarried. She passed away in 1935 in John Street aged only 54 years old.

Z

BORACH ZAFFA

In 1885, Borach Zaffa was living on Queen Street, now Parnell Street. He was one of the growing Jewish community in the city. Many in the community took up residence around the corner in Wolfe Tone Street. The 1901 census of Ireland recorded that there were over 150 individuals of the Jewish faith living in Limerick. Elias Ber Levin, living on Wolfe Tone Street, was the minister to the community for at least ten years.

One of the headstones in the Jewish burial ground in Castletroy. (*Author's collection*)

The Limerick Jewish community grew to such an extent that in 1902 a cemetery for the Lithuanian Jewish community was opened in Castletroy. Among those interred there are Zlato Maissel, whose headstone reads that she died on '5th Nieson 5666' day of the Hebrew Calendar. This was 31 March 1906. Zlato was the wife of Woulfe Maissel, a draper, and lived on Clooney Street.

There were over 122 people of the Jewish faith recorded in the 1911 census as living in Limerick.

Samuel Sochat was living with his son Barnett and his grandchildren at 3 St Joseph's Terrace, off Wolfe Tone Street, when he passed away, aged 70, on 4 March 1917. One of the twelve headstones in the graveyard bears his name. The most recent burial was that of Solomon Sefton, also known as Stuart Clein, who passed away on 2 February 2012.

The graveyard fell into disrepair as the Jewish community slowly left Limerick. In 1990, it was landscaped by Limerick Civil Trust and Limerick Council, who continue to maintain it as a small park.

ZACHARIAH'S LAND AND ZEPP'S CHIPS

In April 1792, Hezekiah Holland passed away at his home on Broad Street. He had been attacked by a gang of robbers on Christmas Eve of the previous year and had never recovered. He bequeathed his land at Crossnagalla to his brother, Zachariah Holland in Killonan. This land came with controversy, leading Zachariah to post an announcement in the *Limerick Chronicle* on 11 November 1793, cautioning people about bidding on lands being auctioned at Crossnagalla, as there were arrears owed to him and he had referred the issue to the Lord Chancellor of Ireland. Zachariah only survived another eight years.

In 1902, German-born Henry Zepp was fined for assaulting Private James Fenton of the 1st Battalion, Royal Irish Regiment. Fenton had gone to buy some chipped potatoes from Zepp and when he put his hand into the boiler they were kept in, Zepp banged the door of the boiler down, catching Fenton's hand. This led to a quarrel, during which the German man struck the soldier on the head with a poker, fracturing his skull. Although Zepp was let off with just a fine, the incident took its toll on the chip maker. Not long after this he entered the District Asylum, where he would reside until his death eleven years later, aged only 38.

Other families with their surname starting with Z arrived in Limerick to work on the Ardnacrusha hydroelectric scheme in the late 1920s. This extraordinary project brought engineers and workers from all over the world. Some of those who arrived in the city brought their future spouses with them. Ernst Zufle, a foreman in Arndacrusha, married Magdalena Sussmeier on 5 March 1927. Twenty-year-old Lucia Zupaucic married Joseph Parderski,

Ardnacrusha Hydro-electric scheme under construction in the 1920s. (*Image courtesy of Siemens-Schuckertwerke*)

an electrician, on 17 September 1927. Wilhelm Zutavern, a fitter, married 20-year-old Frida Erle of 26 Catherine Street on 18 December 1927. Else Zimmermann married August Kupper, a foreman, on 9 October 1929 at the registry office. These couples all returned to their respective countries after the hydroelectric scheme was completed in 1929.

Bibliography

NEWSPAPERS AND JOURNALS

Advocate (Melbourne, Australia)
Anglo-Celt
Cork Examiner
Dublin Evening Mail
Dublin Evening Post
Dublin Weekly Nation
Evening Echo
Evening Herald
Evening Post
Freeman's Journal
Illustrated London News
Irish Examiner
Irish Independent
Irish Life, The Weekly Illustrated Journal of Ireland
Irish Press
Irish Times
Kerryman
Leicestershire Mercury
Limerick and Clare Examiner
Limerick Christmas Gazette
Limerick Chronicle
Limerick Evening Echo
Limerick Leader
Limerick Life
Limerick Magazine
Limerick Post

Limerick Reporter and Tipperary Vindicator
London Evening Standard
Munster Express
Nation
Nenagh Guardian
New Zealand Tablet
North Munster Antiquarian Journal
Old Limerick Journal
Pall Mall Gazette
Sunday Independent
Wellington Independent
Western Times
Yorkshire Gazette
Yorkshire Post and Leeds Intelligencer

OTHER PRIMARY SOURCES

Bassett's Directory of the City and County of Limerick 1875–6 (Limerick: William Bassett, 1877).

Burke, Bernard, *The General Armory of England, Scotland, Ireland, and Wales, Comprising a Registry of Armorial Bearings from the Earliest to the Present Time* (London: Harrison & son, 1884).

Census of Population England, Scotland and Wales, 1841–1911.

Census of Population Ireland, 1821–1911 (Dublin, 1821–1911).

Census of Population Ireland, 1926–2011 (Dublin, 1926–2011).

Dublin, Cork, and South of Ireland: A Literary, Commercial, and Social Review (London: Stratten and Stratten, 1892).

Ferrar, John, *Ferrar's Directory of Limerick,* (Limerick: John Ferrar, 1769).

Francis Guy's Directory of Munster: comprising the counties of Clare, Cork, Kerry, Limerick, Tipperary, and Waterford (Cork: Francis Guy, 1886).

Irish Industrial Yearbook (Dublin: McEvoy Press, 1934–75).

The Limerick City and Counties of Limerick and Clare Directory 1891–92 (Limerick: Ashe, 1891).

The Limerick Directory and Principal Towns in the County of Limerick (Limerick: William Bassett, 1877).

Limerick Petty Sessions Court Records, 1828–1912.

Register of Births, Deaths and Marriages Ireland, 1864–1974.

Register of Deaths England and Wales, 1837–2007.
Slater's Directory of Munster (Dublin: Isaac Slater, 1856).

SECONDARY SOURCES

Bennis, E.H., *Reminiscences of Old Limerick* (Limerick, 1940).
Broderick, David, *The First Toll Roads: Ireland's Turnpike Roads, 1729–1858* (Cork, 2002).
Carroll, Joe, & Touhy, Pat, *Village by the Shannon* (Limerick, 1991).
Connellan, Brendan, *Light on the Past* (Limerick, 2001).
Cosgrove, Art (ed.), *A New History of Ireland, Volume II, Medieval Ireland 1169–1534* (Oxford, 1987).
Donnelly, Kevin, Hoctor, Michael, and Walsh, Dermot, *A Rising Tide, The Story of Limerick Harbour* (Limerick, 1994).
Ferrar, John, *History of Limerick, Ecclesiastical, Civil and Military from the Earliest Records to the Year 1787*, (Limerick, 1787).
Fitzgerald, Rev. Patrick, & McGregor, J.J., *The History, Topography, and Antiquities, of the County and City of Limerick* (Limerick, 1827).
Grealy, Thomas, *St. Mary's Church 1932–1982* (Limerick, 1982).
Hannan, Kevin, *Limerick. Historical Reflections* (Limerick, 1996).
Hill, Judith, *The Building of Limerick* (Cork, 1991).
Hodkinson, Brian J., *The Medieval City of Limerick* (Dublin, 2009).
Irwin, Liam, *The Diocese of Limerick An Illustrated History* (Limerick, 2013).
Joyce, Gerry, *Limerick City Street Names* (Limerick, 1997).
Lee, David, *Remembering Limerick* (Limerick, 1997).
Lee, David, & Jacobs, Debbie (eds.), *Made in Limerick: History of Industries, Trade and Commerce*, Vol. 1 (Limerick, 2003).
Lenihan, Maurice, *History of Limerick* (Cork, reprint, 1967).
Lewis, Samuel, *A Topographical Dictionary of Ireland* (London, 1837).
J. O'Connor, Patrick, *Exploring Limerick's Past. An Historical Geography of Urban Development in County and City* (Newcastle West, 1987).
O'Neill, Timothy, *Merchants and Mariners in Medieval Ireland* (Dublin, 1987).
Potter, Matthew, *First Citizens of the Treaty City* (Limerick, 2007).
Prendergast, Frank, & Seoighe, Mainchin (ed.). *Limerick's Glory* (N. Ireland, 2002).
Slater, Sharon, *The Little Book of Limerick* (Dublin, 2013).
Spellissy, Sean, *The History of Limerick City* (Limerick, 1998).

Spellissy, Sean, *The Rich Land* (Limerick, 1989).
Vaughan, W.E., & Fitzpatrick, A.J. (eds.), *Irish historical statistics population 1821–1971* (Dublin, 1978).

WEBSITES

Ancestry, www.ancestry.co.uk
Dictionary of Irish Biography, https://dib.cambridge.org
National Archives, Census of Ireland 1901/1911, www.census.nationalarchives.ie
Limerick Archives, www.limerick.ie/archives
Limerick Library, www.limerickcity.ie/Library/LocalStudies
Limerick Museum, http://museum.limerick.ie
Limerick's Life, www.limerickslife.com
Historic Graves Project, https://historicgraves.com
Irish Genealogy, www.irishgenealogy.ie
National Inventory of Architectural Heritage, www.buildingsofireland.ie

Index of Places

LIMERICK CITY

LIMERICK COUNTY